Longman/Institute of Housing

The Housing Practice Series

Social Housing and the Social Services

ongman

D1344992

INSTITUTE OF
HOUSING

Paul Spicker

Published by the Institute of Housing (Services) Ltd, Units 15 and 16
Mercia Business Village, Westwood Business Park, Torwood Close,
Coventry CV4 8HX and Longman Group UK Ltd, 6th Floor,
Westgate House, The High, Harlow, Essex, CM20 1YR

Published in the IOH/Longman Housing Practice Series under the General
Editorship of Peter Williams

First published 1989

British Library Cataloguing in Publication Data
Spicker, Paul
 Social housing and the social services.
 — (Housing practice).
 1. Great Britain. Local authority
 housing. Allocation
 I. Title II. Williams, Peter II
 III. Series
 363.5'8

ISBN 0-582-02955-4

Phototypeset by P's & Q's Ltd, 18 Harrington Street, Liverpool L2 9QA
Telephone: 051-236 7953
Printed and bound in Great Britain by
Biddles Ltd, Guildford and King's Lynn

Contents

Preface

This book is an examination of the relationship between social housing and the other main social services. It is intended primarily for use by housing officers and by people training to be housing officers; its purpose is to give some insight into the structure and functions of the social services with which housing officers have to work most closely, the problems of the client groups, and the role of social housing in providing for needs.

The book is more a work in social administration than one in social policy. The distinction between policy and administration has become blurred, and in many cases the narrower focus on administrative issues has been rejected altogether. This is not to underestimate the importance of the study of social policy, which can help to provide explanations for the range of problems examined here. However, the book's aims are more limited; it provides a foundation of knowledge about the social services and their clients which should be of direct interest and use to practitioners.

The material in the book is the result of work over a number of years in the education of housing professionals. Some of this material has featured before in a series of short articles in *Housing*, the journal of the Institute of Housing, and some passages from these articles have been reproduced within the text. They include: 'Social work: a guide for the perplexed', December 1984; 'Is housing a social service?', April 1985; 'Disabled myths', March 1986; 'No place like a home', April 1986, and 'Passing the buck', March 1987.

I have to thank Peter Williams, Professor of Housing Management at UWIST, and Bob Passmore, Housing Manager at Raglan HA, for comments on drafts of the text. Any mistakes are, of course, my own.

About this book
The book has four main sections. It begins by considering the role of housing within the welfare state. The second part reviews the

administrative context — the relationship between housing and social security, health, and the personal social services. Next, it considers the issues of community care, and the special problems of the main client groups — old, disabled, mentally ill and mentally handicapped people, and children in need. By way of conclusion, it discusses the role of social housing in meeting needs, and the effects that changing circumstances are likely to have on housing management.

Part 1 considers the nature of social services and the welfare state, issues of dependency and poverty, and the role of housing as a social service. The purpose of this section is to offer a basic conceptual frame for much of the material which follows, and to place social housing in context. Social housing is becoming residualised, and its role is changing, though the capacity of housing services to cope has been aggravated by a legacy of the problems of the past, under-resourcing, and the spatial concentration of deprivation.

Part 2, on the social services, begins with a consideration of the structure of central and local government through which social services are largely organised and controlled. The chapters which follow deal with the principal social services with which housing services are involved. Each service is described in outline; the chapters address principal issues in their structure and organisation, and their relationship to housing services. The discussion of social security is arguably the most complex area covered in the book. It covers both a description and basic analysis of the social security system as a whole, and an examination of the implications and impact of the benefits. Health services are perhaps less centrally relevant to housing officers than they used to be, when housing was thought of primarily as a service for public health, but the material in this chapter should be of interest in two ways. In the first place, there are direct links between housing and health services, as a result of policies on community care. Secondly, the information about the structure, organisation and finance of health services contains important lessons for social policy. Chapter 6 considers the structure and organisation of personal social services, with particular reference to social work.

Part 3 is concerned with community care, a concept which has significant implications for housing services. Community care is a vague term; I have emphasised within it the importance of enabling people to participate fully as members of a community. The argument made throughout this part of the book is that health, housing, personal social services and social security have to be seen as inter-related, and that housing officers should act in consequence as part of a multi-disciplinary team.

The special problems of the main client groups are examined, with a discussion of how adequately the services meet their needs, and the role of housing in providing for these groups. The primary aim of community services has been to seek to promote independence and 'normalisation'. However, the diversity of people's needs is such that a wide variety of services is required, and people's needs can be met only through the co-operation and co-ordination of a range of different services. This is particularly true of elderly people, who are not by any means an homogenous group; various types of provision have to be offered according to the degree of dependency. Physically disabled people also have very different types of need — relatively few are in wheelchairs, for example — and many services for them are inadequate because they fail to meet the needs. Mental illness and mental handicap have become more important for housing officers in recent years as a result of policies of de-institutionalisation. In both cases, the terms — which themselves describe very different kinds of need — disguise a wide range of conditions and problems; but the range of responses which is available is limited. The focus of policies for children in need has shifted from a general concern with poverty towards a more pathological and individualistic approach. Housing officers can expect to be drawn directly into policies aimed at protecting children at risk.

The final part discusses the changing role of housing management. Housing is essential to social welfare, and the provision of housing a vital part of the welfare state. However, the concept of need widely used in housing is too narrow; housing need has to be seen in the context of needs and provisions overall. Housing management has to change because the context in which it operates is changing. The role of the housing manager has to be redefined, as one which serves disadvantaged people and the wider community in the context of a network of social services.

Part 1
Social housing and the welfare state

Chapter 1
Social services and social welfare

Summary. Housing is a social service. Social services are often associated with 'dependency', but this does not have to be seen in a negative sense; the idea of the 'welfare state' is based on an 'institutional' model of welfare, in which dependency is accepted, or 'institutionalised', as a normal part of social life. Housing is a major element in people's welfare, both as a commodity in itself, and as a determinant of the way people live. Housing has to be seen as a social service not least because it is a crucial part of the welfare state.

The provision of housing is widely viewed as a social service. The other services usually seen in this way are health care, social security, education and social work. This is not by any means an exhaustive list of the 'social services'; it would be possible to include many others, for example, employment, transport, or consumer protection. In many ways, the classification of social services is based in convention, and often it makes little or no obvious sense. Government subsidies to tenants are 'social services', but subsidies to owner-occupiers are not. Job creation is a social service, but the regulation, subsidy and economic control of industry to promote employment is not. The statement that 'housing is a social service' is not, however, just an arbitrary classification. It carries a set of implications about the nature and purposes of housing provision. Richard Titmuss, one of the most influential thinkers in social policy, argued that:

> The definition, for most purposes, of what is a social service should take its stand on aims; not on the administrative methods and institutional devices employed to achieve them (1955, p.42).

This is not an easy task; the aims of social services are complex. Clearly, part of their aim is to benefit individuals — by delivering goods or services, sometimes by 'treating' people with problems, or perhaps, like education, developing each person's capabilities. But they can also have a social, as well as an individual, focus, acting as a means of changing society, or as mechanisms of social control. In general terms, the social services are mainly concerned with the welfare of the individual and society.

Perhaps the most important defining element of a social service is that it is redistributive: the people who benefit from it are not necessarily the people who have paid. There are other collective services of which the same could be said. 'Public' services include roads, transport, water, parks and libraries. The difference seems to be that although everyone uses public services, or at least stands to benefit from them, social services go only to people in 'need'. But this distinction is more than a little arbitrary; people 'need' a public water supply at least as much as they 'need' state education. The importance of it is that the recipients of social services are seen as dependent in a way in which users of public services are not. Medical care is a social service because it deals with sickness; education, with children; social security, with poverty, unemployment and old age. The difference between housing and water supply is that we classify public tenants as 'dependent' without applying the term to people who turn on the tap.

In part, the distinction between public services and social services is made because social services have a *residual* function — acting as a safety net when other methods fail. Eyden defines a social service as

> a social institution that has developed to meet the personal needs of individual members of society not adequately or effectively met by either the individual from his own or his family's resources or by commercial or industrial concerns (Byrne & Padfield 1978, p.1).

This seems too limited. Social services are not concerned only with individuals: they also provide for families, groups, and communities. And some social services, like health or education, are provided for everyone, even though some of the needs they deal with might be met by other resources that people have.

The main alternative to the residual view of welfare is *institutional* welfare. Titmuss refers to 'states of dependency' which are recognised as collective responsibilities. (1955, pp.42-43) These include injury, disease, disability, old age, childhood, maternity and unemployment. Everyone is likely to be a child, old, or ill at some time. Dependency is accepted, or 'institutionalised', as a normal part of social life; the institutional model of welfare attempts to extend social responsibility to cover all the circumstances in which dependency is likely to arise. When this view is taken, the distinction between public services and social services collapses; we all have needs for which the community, and not the individual, must provide.

The idea of institutional welfare is closely linked with the idea of the 'welfare state'. Briggs outlines three ways in which the welfare state affects social relationships:

> First by guaranteeing individuals and families a minimum income irrespective of the market value of their work, or their property. Second by narrowing the extent of insecurity by enabling individuals and families to meet certain 'social

contingencies' (for example sickness, old age and unemployment) which lead otherwise to individual or family crisis, and third, by ensuring that all citizens without distinction of status or class are offered the best standards available in relation to a certain agreed range of social services (1961, pp.228-230).

The first two criteria could apply to residual social services; it is the third which distinguishes the 'welfare state' from other types of social provision. It makes two points. One is that the service should be at the best possible level. The other is the principle of universality, that services should cover everyone. This principle was central to the foundation of the British Welfare State, as represented in the National Health Service and the Beveridge Report; it is what distinguished the welfare state from the Poor Law and other social services which came before it.

Dependency

John Moore, the Secretary of State for Social Security, has suggested in a widely reported speech that 'The next step forward in the long evolutionary march of the welfare state in Britain is away from dependence and towards independence'. Moore argues, following similar debates in the US, that the welfare state has inculcated a 'culture of dependency'. In one sense, this is true. The welfare state is founded in the view that dependency — or, to put it in more positive terms, interdependence, for we depend on each other — is a natural and normal part of social existence. The opposition to 'dependency' is based, in part, in a residual view of welfare, and in part in a belief that dependency is morally reprehensible — a condition, in Moore's words, 'corrupting of the human spirit'.

The concept of 'dependency' is unfortunately plagued with negative implications. But there are many different kinds of 'dependency', and they are not all to be condemned. Children, old people, and sick people are all 'dependent' in one sense or another. A person can be physically dependent, in the sense of relying on the support of others to fulfil certain physical functions, like moving, dressing, or bathing. A person can be psychologically dependent, by needing the intellectual or emotional support of others. And people can be financially dependent, relying on others for financial support. These different kinds of dependency are often confused; the assumption is made that a person who is dependent in one sense is likely to be dependent in others. It may happen — young children are dependent in every sense — but it does not have to; a person can be financially dependent without being psychologically dependent, and a person who is financially independent may be unable to act without calling on others. The identification of the two states, though it is perennially popular in political debate, is based on a crude fallacy. Physical or financial dependency may give someone the power to act, and therefore the degree of psychological independence, which is crucial to their welfare. Interdependence is, for many, the key to independence.

The causes of dependency are not simple. There are, however, some broad classifications of explanation for dependency. Dependency can be seen, first, as *pathological*, related to the inadequacies of the individual who is dependent. A number of conditions are seen as either the fault of the individual, or because the individual is unable to cope, sometimes as both simultaneously. People are unemployed or homeless, by this account, because they are lazy, feckless or incompetent. One of the more extreme examples of this view is found in the idea of the 'problem family', an idea which is still, regrettably, current within housing services. Macey and Baker point to three common characteristics — rent arrears, neglect of the property, and annoyance to neighbours. These are issues which, they acknowledge, are found with other 'unsatisfactory tenants'; problem families represent the worst cases. The authors argue that:

> Apart from a few borderline cases, all these problem families exhibit one common factor, namely, their inability to cope with their circumstances (1982, p.433).

It would be wrong to pretend that families which have this range of characteristics do not exist, but some words of caution are needed. When people refer to 'problem families', they do not usually mean to say that they are people who have problems. They mean families who cause problems for other people, which is quite a different proposition. Macey suggests that

> it may sometimes be desirable to move a family from a good post-war dwelling to a less desirable one and to 'promote' them to better accommodation as they respond to persuasion (1982, p.437).

The idea that people who are 'unable to cope' will 'respond to persuasion' by punitive measures is a contradiction in terms; it comes from a confusion between two very different issues. Being from a 'problem family' means that assumptions are made about the behaviour of an individual which may be very damaging to that individual. The term 'problem family' is, then, a stigmatising label.

The second set of explanations for dependency are *sub-cultural* — the product of a social environment. Explanations of this sort were very popular in the 1960s, when Oscar Lewis argued that a 'culture of poverty' was producing deviant behaviour in slum areas (see e.g. Lewis, 1968). The attraction of sub-cultural explanations is that they seem to explain why certain social problems are likely to be concentrated in specific geographical areas or communities. In the United States, Lewis's theory was influential in the establishment of urban policy, which in turn later influenced urban policy in Britain. The observation is, however, based on a confusion; the problems are indeed likely to occur in the same areas, but it does not mean that they are likely to be manifested by the same people. This is still, at root, an explanation which puts the responsibility for dependency on the people who are dependent, and Lewis's arguments were attacked in part because of the political position they represented, and in part for the lack of good evidence to support them (see e.g. Valentine 1968, Townsend 1979).

Third, there are *structural* explanations for dependency, which attribute dependency to the structure of the society in which it takes place.

People are unemployed and financially dependent, not because of their individual deficiencies, but because of the economic structure of society which is unable to provide them with useful employment. People are unemployed because there are not enough jobs; people are homeless because there are not enough houses. In any competition for resources, some people are going to lose; the problem rests, not with the losers, but in the necessity for competition. Old people or disabled people are dependent, not because they are incapable of doing anything, but because of a 'social construction' of dependency, by which the things which they can do are devalued and disregarded. Structural explanations do not necessarily exclude pathological ones; it still needs to be explained which people are most likely to be vulnerable, or to be excluded within a competitive society. What they do is to shift the emphasis, and ask whether it is appropriate to centre on individualistic solutions to social problems, or to blame the casualties and victims of the social structure for their condition.

It is possible to link these different concepts to different models of welfare. The pathological and sub-cultural views are linked to a residual model of welfare; welfare provision is a 'safety net' for people who have failed in a competitive society. Structural explanations are linked to the institutional model. If dependency is created by society, then it is the responsibility of society to care for the people who are made dependent by it, and to seek to empower them to act independently as far as possible.

Poverty

The concepts of welfare and poverty are closely linked. Welfare is, in its simplest sense, a person's 'well-being'; the idea is linked to the provision of services because the services are intended to improve people's circumstances. Poverty is the lack of material resources, a condition which is antithetical to well-being. The social services are centrally concerned with issues of poverty, for two reasons. In the first place, poverty creates, or at least exacerbates, many of the problems which social services have to deal with, for example, through stress, disease, social isolation, or a poor environment. Secondly, even though social services may have universalist aspirations, in practice the people who are served are often those who have no other alternative. In theory, anybody may be homeless; in practice, the people most vulnerable are those who are unable to afford any alternative or who are already in the least satisfactory housing. Over 60% of council and housing association tenants are on benefits. In the case of social work, Becker and MacPherson (1988) found that despite a myth of the universal availability of personal social services, 90% of the clients of social workers were in receipt of benefits.

There are two main concepts of poverty. *Absolute poverty* is based on subsistence, a minimum standard needed to live. Seebohm Rowntree, writing at the turn of the century, distinguished *primary poverty,* having less than necessary for subsistence, from *secondary poverty,* when one finishes without enough because of the way that money has been spent. His purpose in doing so was to counter the right-wing argument that people were poor because they failed to manage their money properly; he showed that even if they managed it perfectly, on an extremely restrictive standard, many people would still be in primary poverty.

Relative poverty is based on a comparison of poor people with others in society. A person who might be considered 'poor' in Britain would be 'well off' in the Third World. 'Relative' poverty relates this to inequality, and the circumstances enjoyed by others. The main advocate of relative poverty is Peter Townsend, who defines it as

> the absence or inadequacy of those diets, amenities, standards, services and activities which are common or customary in society (1979, p.915).

This is not quite good enough as a definition of poverty, because it confuses poverty with deprivation; one can be deprived without being poor. The issue is that there is a level below which the absence of these things is considered especially serious, and this level is socially defined.

Most commentators agree that poverty is socially defined, but this does not necessarily mean that it is 'relative' in Townsend's sense. An absolute standard might define poverty mainly in terms of a lack of food, clothing, fuel and shelter, but it is evident that the way these elements are defined has to depend on social conditions. For example, there is undoubtedly some nutritional value in eating cats, dogs, or insects, but as a general proposition these options are rarely available to people living in the United Kingdom. The same is true of other basic 'essentials'. Adequate clothing is assessed in terms of decency and convenience, not only in terms of warmth and protection. The fuel that is necessary depends on the conditions in which the fuel is used. And the definition of what is a 'shelter' equally is different in different societies, a function not only of climate and materials, but also land tenure and the social organisation of housing. In the Third World, squatting is a widespread, and arguably a 'normal', form of tenure. But a person in Britain who is without a home does not have the option of erecting a squatter shack, not so much because of the lack of materials, as the limitations of land use and the restrictions of the law. A person who attempts to squat (in the sense in which people squat in Nigeria or Colombia, rather than in Bayswater) is likely to be moved on and have the place demolished. And a person who is literally homeless — on the street, without any accommodation at all — is liable, not just to be moved on, but to be arrested. It doesn't seem in the least forced to describe this as a clearly defined minimum level, which people are not supposed to fall below. But it is equally clear that it is a socially defined condition, because the circumstances which produce it are necessarily social. The idea of a socially produced minimum was, incidentally, the position taken by Marx; and in the USSR, people are considered to be poor by an absolute standard which shifts according to social conditions (McAuley 1977).

Command over resources
Poverty is mainly to do with a lack of resources. A person's financial

resources are usually considered either as wealth or as income. The difference between them is that wealth is a stock, or holding, and income a flow — a way of representing the resources likely to be available in the short term.

To consider income without wealth can be misleading. Two families on benefit will have very different experiences if one has carpets, curtains, household items and a fridge, and the other has no furniture, no household items and no adequate stock of clothes. This is true in part because the second family will have to spend money to make up for the things they lack; they will often spend more on heating, because they lack warm clothes and furnishings, and more on food, because it cannot be stored and has to be bought in smaller quantities. In part, too, it happens because income and wealth are simply different ways of looking at the same thing. If the family which has possessions and household items needs something in particular, like a pullover, a screwdriver, a pair of scissors, they will take it out of storage; the family that does not have the stock of things will have to go out and buy them.

Although on the face of it wealth appears to be more important for welfare than income, there are problems in using wealth as an indicator. In the first place, wealth is difficult to measure. What value does one put on a person's clothing, shoes, cutlery, or bedding? Secondly, from the point of view of welfare, the question of formal ownership is of much less interest than the question of use. A family which owns its house has an accumulating capital asset, but it cannot realistically hope to sell it and live off the proceeds. A council tenant may well make a similar use of a house to an owner-occupier. There are advantages in owner-occupation — like the ability to improve one's circumstances, to develop the property, and to leave capital to one's children — but it is questionable whether a person's wealth, measured by the capital value of assets, is a very good guide to the actual difference in welfare.

Even if both income and wealth are considered, poverty is not simply a question of money. Money is used as an indicator of a person's material lifestyle, and that depends on *command over resources*. A child in a wealthy family is not necessarily rich, but he or she may be able to draw on the family's resources. A person in a high status occupation may be able to draw on credit facilities even though current resources are limited. Conversely, a person living in a poor area may not be able to obtain credit, to order a taxi, or to have milk delivered.

Housing and welfare

Housing is a major determinant of a person's material conditions. Most people in Britain now live in a state of relative affluence. At the same time, many people lack items which are widely considered essential.

Possession of durable goods by households, 1985

	% households with children	% all households
Fridge	97	95
Deep freeze	78	66
Washing machine	95	81
Tumble drier	51	33
Telephone	81	81
TV	99	97
Video	48	31

[Households without children are mainly pensioners, single people and childless couples.]

An index of deprivation (Mack and Lansley, 1985)

	Described as essential by (%)	Unable to afford (%)
Heating	97	6
Indoor toilet	96	1
Damp free home	96	8
Bath	94	2
Public transport	88	3
Warm waterproof coat	87	7
3 meals a day for children	82	4
Self-contained accommodation	79	3
2 pairs of all-weather shoes	78	11
Enough bedrooms for children	77	10
Refrigerator	77	1
Toys for children	71	3
Carpets	70	3
Celebrations on special occasions like Xmas	69	4
Roast joint or equivalent once a week	67	7
Washing machine	67	5

[This table probably underestimates the extent of deprivation. Some of the people who cannot afford goods will say that they don't need them, either because they are ashamed to admit their poverty, or because they are genuinely used to a lower standard of living than the rest of the population.]

The relationship of these factors to housing is fairly clear. The first four factors in the table are conventionally considered as 'housing' issues, and housing accounts for six of the top ten. Other factors are related indirectly to housing — transport facilities depend in large part on location; a refrigerator has now replaced the traditional housing requirement for 'facilities for the storage of food'; and the installation of a washing machine depends not only on finance, but also on the amount of space available, and on plumbing facilities.

In many ways, bad housing is one of the simplest and clearest indicators of poverty — the condition in which people most clearly lack material welfare. This is largely because housing is a commodity in itself, and as such one of the most important resources for people to command. If people have the money, they are likely to use it to some degree to improve their housing conditions.

Housing is more, though, than a commodity. It is also a major determinant of the way people live. Housing affects people's lifestyle — what they do when they are by themselves, what pursuits and activities they undertake. It affects their social relationships, which depend strongly on issues such as location, facilities for entertainment, and social status. As such, housing is a fundamental element of people's welfare.

Social housing

The idea of 'social housing' is not commonly used in the United Kingdom, though the term would be immediately recognised by people involved in the provision of housing in most of Europe. It refers to housing as a social service, that is, on a collective social basis, by the state, or by voluntary organisations.

If housing is to be seen as a social service, it is for three main reasons. In the first place, provision is being made for dependent groups. The provision of social housing was initially intended for the the 'working classes'; social housing was a massive response to a massive social issue.

As housing conditions have improved, and policies have changed, the focus has shifted to those people who are unable to find satisfactory accommodation in the private sector. This includes people who have financial difficulties, people who have particular problems of access through discrimination or lack of resources, and many others who have particular needs for 'community care' — the client groups considered in the third part of this book.

Secondly, the methods which housing officers are called on to employ are similar to those used by other social services. Housing cannot be divorced from the other functions of social care. The problems which housing officers are facing require not only the specific skills and knowledge base necessary for the management of property, but also a developed competence in the skills of working with people — for example, assessment, communication, interviewing and building relationships — which are fundamental to social service provision.

Third, and perhaps most important, the aims of social housing are the aims of a social service. Although the activities of social services can be interpreted in many ways, at the simplest level social services are concerned with the care and support of the members of a society, either as individuals, or in ways which benefit groups, communities and the whole society. Housing is crucial to a person's welfare; social housing exists to meet one of the most basic human needs.

The association of social services with dependency means that there may be a negative implication in the idea that housing is a social service, and some housing professionals may be reluctant to accept the label. But the idea does not commit the service to a narrow concept of 'welfarism' or residual provision. It identifies housing, rather, with the aims and aspirations of the welfare state. It helps to alert the providers of the service to the complex nature of their responsibilities towards the people who look to social housing for assistance. And it stresses that housing is a basic need, which requires social provision in order to guarantee adequate standards.

Chapter 2
Social housing

Summary. Social housing developed in large part as a universal service, though it has always had important residual elements. It is now being 'residualised', with major changes in the profile of its tenants, who are more likely to be poor or to have special needs. The poverty of the tenants leads to important social problems, which council housing has been ill-equipped to deal with; the service has a legacy of problems and under-resourcing. However, social housing is still a highly appropriate method of dealing with people who are most in need, and it has a major role to play within the welfare state.

Social housing in Britain has developed primarily as local authority housing, and an understanding of its role depends largely on the position of council housing. Before the First World War, the provision of housing was not a significant element in social policy; there were about 10,000 council houses in total. The change brought about by the 1919 Addison Act was substantial. The Act's main aims were to provide housing for the 'working classes'; to create 'homes fit for heroes'; and, one might note, to put off the threat of a Bolshevik revolution (see Orbach 1977). The Act represented a major development towards a universalist service. It gave a subsidy to local authorities equivalent to the cost of the housing less the product of a penny on the rates. This was a blank cheque to local authorities, and did not last long. New subsidies in 1923 and 1924 meant that houses built in the 1920s were of a fairly good standard, though they often lacked modern amenities. With the Greenwood Act of 1930, council housing became more concerned with replacing housing being removed by clearance, and after 1935, with reducing overcrowding. By 1939, about two million houses had been built.

After the war, the role of council housing grew further; the emphasis fell primarily on the replacement of the housing stock, with mass building often to a very inferior standard compared with the inter-war period. Quantity was more important than quality. The subsidies favoured high-rise building and development of expensive sites. The largest booms were during the early 1950s, with Macmillan as Minister of Housing, and under the Labour Government 1964-70, which was committed to building half a million houses a year, a target it never achieved. The boom ended in 1972. The Conservative government of the time introduced a Housing Finance Act which reduced general subsidies, trebling rents, and introduced rent rebates for people in need. The general principle of transferring subsidy from houses to individual tenants was equally adopted by the Conservative government after 1979.

The 1970s and 80s have seen, then, a major change in the relationship of social housing to the welfare state. Council housing was originally developed, as noted above, as housing for the 'working classes'. When the welfare state was introduced, the reference to the 'working classes' was removed from the legislation, in keeping with the aim to make provision universal. Since 1972, however, the move has been away from universal provision and subsidy for general needs, and has concentrated instead on providing support for individuals. Council housing has been described as becoming 'residualised' — that is, a service acting as a safety net, rather than as a universal or institutional service.

It is important to recognise, however, that council housing has actually had a major residual role for many years. In the first place, council housing was used during the 1930s for rehousing of people from slum housing and overcrowded households. This meant, in the normal course of events, that the people moving into council housing could reasonably be expected to represent a relatively poorer stratum of society. It is difficult in retrospect to substantiate the case, but it seems intrinsically unlikely that the effect of mass clearance post war was to make the occupancy of council housing more representative socially. Clearance largely affected the worst housing, and in the situation of a market the people who would occupy the worst housing would tend to be those with the least command over resources. It would follow from this that council housing, and in particular newly constructed council housing, would contain families who were relatively poor. However, the post-war trend was for young families to have at least one and perhaps two main earners, and for the majority of poor children to cease to be poor by the time they became adults. In effect, then, the allocation of property to poor families did not necessarily imply residualisation of council housing overall. The effect of these developments was often to lead to substantial distinctions between different estates. Although many council estates were settled estates, with long-term residents on middling incomes, there have consistently been a number of council houses which, for one reason or another, have been less settled, less desirable and less easy to live in than others.

The principal effect of 'residualisation' has been a major shift in the profile of council tenants. Subsidies to council housing have been progressively removed; many councils now make a profit on their rents. The subsidies have been replaced by personal benefits; perhaps 60% of council tenants receive Housing Benefit. (The figure before April 1988 was nearer to 75%, which indicates that many tenants who do not qualify for Housing Benefit nevertheless have low incomes.) The withdrawal of general subsidy, and the sale of council housing at a discount, have encouraged the better-off tenants to buy houses instead. It is difficult to say how much effect this has had on the level of owner occupation — many of those who have bought their council houses may have moved into owner-occupation anyway — but it has had the effect both of creaming off richer tenants, and reducing the stock available to deal with general needs. Potential tenants are more likely to buy instead of renting. The main reason now why people apply for council housing is that they cannot afford a satisfactory alternative (DoE 1988).

The process of residualisation has led, to some extent, to a greater emphasis on housing as a social service, in the sense of a service which is concentrating on people who are dependent. There has been an increasing emphasis on allocations to people in need, and in particular on homeless families and elderly people. However, it has also had the effect of reducing the capacity of council housing to respond to need, because there are fewer houses available for letting, because the houses which remain are of lower quality, and because the problems of many of the tenants require resources which the local authorities do not have. The central argument against residual services is that they may become second-class services, representing a basic division in society — a development fundamentally opposed to the principle of a 'welfare state'.

The impact of poverty

The increasing poverty of the tenants has had a substantial impact on the character of social housing, and many housing problems have to be understood in the context of that poverty. For example, heating is, for most people on benefit, the major expense after rent and food, and the cost of attempting to maintain adequate heating adds to the financial problems of poor people. Ventilation has been inadequate — modern houses tend to be sealed against drafts, and unflued heating systems are widely used because they are cheap to install. The common result is a problem with condensation. Poor households cannot afford a level of heat which can avoid it.

Poverty is equally likely to be associated with a range of social problems. Research in Liverpool (Flynn et al 1972) found extremely high associations between the following problems in different wards of the city, which means that where one is found, the others are likely to be found too. The indicators include theft, possession orders, warrants for disconnection of electricity, children being deloused, unemployment, assault, welfare conference cases, burglary, debtors, miscellaneous crimes, adults mentally ill, malicious damage (vandalism), children ESN (educationally sub-normal), and job instability. These associations are based on parts of a city, not on individuals; there is no evidence to suggest that the problems are particularly likely to be found in the same households. Most of these associations are directly attributable to poverty. Unemployment, job instability, adults being mentally ill are causes of poverty. Theft and burglary, possession orders, disconnections, debt are consequences of it —

one should note that people in poor areas are more likely to be the victims of crime. Most of the other factors can be explained indirectly in similar terms; children may be ESN — or, to use a less pejorative term, slow learners — because their parents are intellectually handicapped, and live in these areas because their incomes are low; there is more vandalism because there are inadequate facilities to play at home; there is more attention from the police and welfare agencies.

It is not the case that poverty is only found within limited areas, in fact, most poor people do not live in poor areas (Barnes & Lucas 1975); nor would it be true to say that all of these problems are found exclusively in public sector housing. But clearly, the tenants of social housing are poorer than others (see DoE 1988); and, within the public sector, poverty and the problems associated with it are more likely to be found in certain areas. There are several reasons for this. The concentration of poor people in certain areas has been attributed to deliberate segregation. Public housing managers have 'graded' tenants according to their standards of housekeeping and suitability as prospective tenants (see e.g. Duke 1970, Simpson 1981); the practice is commended by Macey and Baker, which has been for too long the principal text in housing management (Macey 1984). Although grading has fallen out of favour in recent years, it has left a legacy that is likely to continue for some time.

Deliberate segregation is not crucial to an understanding of the social divisions in housing. The same sorts of problems are found in the poorest parts of the private sector. In part, the concentration of deprivation reflects the way towns are structured. Communities are established at different periods. Standards vary according to the age and quality of the stock, and the level of investment devoted to maintenance and improvement. The pattern of employment, and so the resources available to the community, reflect commercial and industrial developments. Within specific areas, the age of the estate and the extent to which settled residence has been established are liable to be reflected in the structure of the community.

However, the main root of social disadvantage lies in the magic of the market. Poor people have been concentrated in the worst housing, because it is poor people who have the most limited command over resources, and have least choice as to where they can go. The same mechanism applies in the public sector. Research in Glasgow (Clapham & Kintrea 1986) shows that where applicants for council housing are allowed a choice, the people most able to exercise it are those who have the highest incomes and the best housing previously. They are the ones who can wait for a better offer. The worst property has to be allocated to someone, and there is little point in offering it to people who will certainly reject it. The actions of public sector housing officers in separating out types and classes are not so much a cause of spatial differentiation as a recognition of it.

These processes are reflected directly in the occupation of housing in particular estates. The effect of social and spatial segregation is that people who are poorest, most desperate and most vulnerable are substantially more likely to live in accommodation which other people wish to reject, for whatever reason. The sorts of problems commonly associated with these estates — a bad reputation, environmental decline, and social problems — are all reasons why people should choose to live elsewhere. For those who live on the estates, there is a vicious cycle of poverty. Poor people have a limited command of resources, and as a result they are likely to find themselves living in areas with other poor people, often in the worst housing. The condition of the housing, the expense of trying to cope with inadequate heating systems, the problems of living in poor areas, are likely to make the problems of poverty worse.

The problems of local authority housing

The current problems of local authority housing have to be seen in the context of the poverty of the tenants.

1. Stigma
The stigma of council housing probably dates from the 1930s, when the emphasis was on rehousing tenants from the worst slums and severe overcrowding. A number of estates were considered to be socially undesirable from the time of their construction (Tucker 1966). Although the extent to which public housing in Britain is segregated and rejected has never been as great as in, say, the US (see Huttman 1969), it is still true that social divisions have been made between public and private housing, to the extent where many council estates are physically segregated from private areas (see e.g. Collison 1963, or Tucker 1966; the practice has left an evident legacy). The residualisation of council housing, as the better housing within the public sector is sold off and poorer people are concentrated in the remaining stock, exacerbates the general trend.

2. Design + construction
The problems of design and construction in council housing are notorious. On the face of it, the standards of council housing improved over time, with the Dudley report of 1944 offering higher standards of space and amenities than Tudor-Walters in 1918, and Parker-Morris leading to further substantive improvements (Burnett 1978). However, the standards are not the only factor to take into account. When Parker-Morris was adopted in the early 1960s, one of the effects of the apparently higher standards was to create problems of attempting to meet the criteria within cost constraints, which often led to corners being cut.

The crucial element in determining the type and quality of building was the subsidy available for construction. The development of industrial building in the 1950s and 60s did not reflect only the fashions of the time or a 'Utopian dream' — the accusation made by Alice Coleman (1985) — but also the economics of housing construction in view of the subsidy arrangements that had been made. The abolition in 1956 of general needs subsidy for low rise dwellings was an important contributory factor to the growth of high-rise. The Housing Cost Yardstick, introduced in 1967, had a major influence on the pattern of development in the 1970s, tending to favour high-density developments. The capacity of heating systems had to be nominally high, but the installation of flued systems is expensive. The result was often to favour unflued systems that involved relatively low investment, like electric fires, which were cheap to install but expensive for poor families to run, and which, because they provided neither adequate heat nor adequate ventilation, have contributed to many of the problems of condensation in council property.

A further implication in practice of the subsidy arrangements was the emphasis on construction of 'family' housing with either two or three bedrooms. Single units of accommodation tend to be fairly expensive on a per capita basis, because of the need to provide basic amenities; but four bedroomed properties have been consistently difficult to build within cost constraints, and larger houses have hardly been built at all. The time that large families have to wait for council housing, and the difficulty in transferring to other property, reflect the shortage of alternative accommodation.

3. Planning
Many council estates are in isolated locations and lack essential facilities. The location of estates depends largely on the availability of land and its cost; the creation of large estates on the peripheries of cities reflected this constraint. The provision of adequate facilities in such locations depends on the size of the estate: it may be estimated, for example, that a sub post office or chemist requires a catchment area of at least 8000 people (these figures are drawn from planning documents for Telford New Town and Peterborough Development Corporation). A few estates are large enough to support facilities of this kind, but many are not; and shops and services require not only a basic catchment area but also a level of custom from the population served. Shop units provided in council estates for essential services are left unoccupied, or let out to hairdressers and fish and chip shops which need a much smaller catchment area to pay. Even among the largest estates it is unlikely that there will be enough people to support a district shopping centre (which is likely to require at least 24,000 people). Council tenants are also likely to be poorer than others in the population at large, which means that the numbers of people required to support basic facilities are greater than would otherwise be the case. The problem, then, lies more in the economics of the situation than in the actions of town planners.

4. The failure of repair services
Maintenance and repairs are not, strictly speaking, always the responsibility of housing management within the local authority, but they are an essential part of the relationship between landlord and tenant. Reynolds, in her study of a problem housing estate, notes that 'repairs and maintenance . . . caused more resentment than any other problem' (1986, p.32). There are major problems in many areas, apparently through the failure of councils adequately to organise the work.

These problems have to be seen in the context of the conditions in which local authority housing operates. The scale of repairs required, both because of issues of design and construction and also because of years of cumulative under-resourcing, is far beyond what the local authorities are able to cope with. The maintenance functions themselves are under-resourced; local authorities are liable to pay workers less than private firms and frequently do not hold an adequate stock of materials. Moreover, many of the problems of maintenance reflect the poverty of the tenants. Tenants are likely to rely on maintenance by housing services even for relatively simple tasks, like changing a tap washer or easing a door. The costs may seem small, but it is important to realise that many families have no money at all for such tasks.

The demands for maintenance and repair are simply greater than local authorities can cope with with their present level of resources. It is clear that other organisations have been more successful in arranging the maintenance of property, but this is because they have more to do it with. The formation of a co-operative in Possil, Glasgow, to modernise a deprived area was justified in part by the availability of funds which were not available to the local authority. The tenants's report said:

> There is no money for improving council houses, yet there is money to improve privately owned houses. The only way to get the houses improved is to become part of the private sector (*Guardian*, 25.11.84).

5. Under-resourcing
Council housing now faces growing problems. The stock is deteriorating, and the condition of much of the property is such that major repairs need to be done. The Association of Metropolitan Authorities have estimated that over £8,000 million is required for the modernisation and repair of traditional pre-war stock; a further £7,000 million for other traditional housing; £5,000 million for concrete dwellings, and between £3,750 and £5,000 million for industrially built housing (Cantle 1986). Money for new building is limited to the point of non-existence. The subsidy to council tenants has been progressively reduced, and the burden transferred to housing benefit. Management has to cope with new responsibilities; in the course of the last twelve years, these have included, for example, the formation of housing investment programmes, several changes in the structure of housing finance, tenant consultation, the legislation on homelessness, the right to buy, the transfer of local authority estates and the administration of housing benefit.

The future of social housing

The government is now committed to running down council housing. As a first step, council houses have been sold with generous discounts. The second stage is that tenants are being given the 'opportunity' to transfer to other landlords, though the terms of the legislation are such that tenants will be transferred unless they actually oppose the move.

In this process, housing associations have come to be of increasing importance. Housing associations are often referred to as the 'voluntary housing movement'. They have voluntary committees, and many are registered as charities. Like the council sector, most of the tenants receive housing benefit, but this figure conceals important differences. The profile of housing association tenants is not the same as that of local authority tenants. There are many more old people, and people with special needs.

Though housing associations are generally small in comparison with local authorities, they have grown rapidly in recent years, and have attracted the main funding for the construction of social housing. They are mainly funded through the Housing Corporation, a government quango, although they often receive some element of local authority funding and are required to give local authorities a proportion of lettings as a result. As comprehensive housing services, with much more generous funding of management and development than local authorities, they have been able to pioneer changes in practice in housing management.

The housing association movement has received political support from all sides, as an alternative to local authorities, which are seen as excessively large and bureaucratic. This is surprising, because on the face of it housing associations are less efficient than local authorities; they have more intensive management of a smaller number of properties, often spread out over a wide area. What they are able to do is to provide a comprehensive housing service, in a way which most local authority housing departments have not been able to do.

Housing associations have never really been subjected to critical examination. For example, many housing associations have been extremely conservative in their policies, reflecting the practical constraints on small organisations which cannot afford to take financial risks. I think it could be argued legitimately that, in general, housing association management has been more successful than council housing. Housing association properties are generally new or newly improved, built to more generous standards than local authority property, often built in locations where they are mixed with private housing, and usually built on the small scale. Housing associations have had a lot more money for management than local authorities; there are often more staff to each tenant. And a number of associations, like Anchor and Hanover, are performing specialised functions, different in kind from the role of local authorities. But if tenants seem to be more satisfied in some housing association property than in council property, it is important to ask whether like is being compared with like. None of this constitutes evidence that housing associations could perform better than local authorities under the same constraints.

The future of social housing is unclear. Reardon (1988) characterises the government's current housing policy as implying less council housing, greater tenant choice, increased supply through 'independent' landlords, targeting public money on those most in need, either through individual provisions (housing benefit, or improvement grants) or estate action, and the continued growth of owner occupation. The government has argued that local authorities should seek, as far as possible, to withdraw from the provision of public housing. The role of the local authorities, in the White Paper, is seen primarily as facilitators and enablers within the housing market, rather than as direct providers. The picture seems to be one, not simply where local authorities have a diminished role, but where they may cease to provide housing altogether. A large number of authorities are considering protecting their position by the transfer of their stock into housing associations created for the purpose, though this process, at the time of writing, is proving problematic.

On the other hand, the government is prepared to support housing associations, apparently on the basis that housing associations are part of a pluralistic, 'independent' sector in housing. But it is also true that the role of housing associations is not primarily conceived in the terms of social service. The Griffiths report on community care, of which more later, does not mention them at all. Housing associations are being encouraged to seek private finance, a strategy which depends largely on the government's willingness to pay rents through Housing Benefit. The government's attitude towards housing associations seems to show a misunderstanding of the nature of social housing. Once the government has disposed of the public sector, it is going to wake up to the fact that housing associations are, to a large extent, publicly funded; that most of the tenants are on benefits; and that the movement has clear social aims. The housing associations are next in line.

Whatever the government's aspirations, it seems highly unlikely that local authorities will cease to be involved in the provision of housing in the near future. The problem is, simply, that there are too many houses in poor condition, with too many poor tenants, to leave many options for manoeuvre. A change of tenure is no guarantee that social problems can be made to disappear.

Although the role of social housing has diminished, it clearly does still have a major part to play within the welfare state. It is still a mass provision, catering for a wide range of needs and circumstances; for many people, it is the main, perhaps the only, opportunity they are likely to have for adequate housing. It is uniquely able to respond to the needs of the wider society, which is why an increasing emphasis in social housing has fallen on planning, needs assessment and resource allocation. It offers a high degree of security to those who are most deprived, and most likely to be disadvantaged in a competitive market. Social housing is able to provide a range and flexibility of provision which is not always available within the private sector. And it has a major role in helping tenants with special problems and needs, such as people who are physically disabled, very elderly, children at risk, mentally ill and mentally handicapped people — the groups which I propose to concentrate on in the course of this book.

Part 2
The social services

Chapter 3
The administrative framework

Summary. Social housing has, like other services, been organised mainly under the aegis of central and local government. The framework of services is dominated to a large extent by financial controls, and administrative structures have been developed to respond to economic priorities. However, the effect of the administrative structures has made the planning and co-ordination services difficult. Interaction between the services depends on approaches to need which cut across the service boundaries.

Co-ordination and conflict

The importance of the role of housing in the welfare state means, not unnaturally, that housing services are likely to come into contact with other social services in a variety of contexts, and at several different levels. This is particularly true because of an increasing emphasis on groups who are disadvantaged, and those who have special needs. It does not follow, simply because people have needs, that the needs have to be met by services working in concert; people need food and water, but no-one thinks it is necessary to co-ordinate water authorities and grocery stores. Co-ordination is necessary, first, because the clients themselves are not always able to ensure that they receive the services; and the onus of organising the delivery of services has been accepted, to a large degree, as part of the principle of the welfare state. Second, the services are not truly independent of each other. The provision of domiciliary and residential care by social services requires at least some consideration of the provision of accommodation. Most tenants in social housing now depend in large part on social security payments for their rent. Because of the interdependence of the services, they can help each other to achieve their aims — and equally, if there is not adequate co-ordination, they can also hinder each other. Third, beyond the aims of the specific services, there are the broader social aims associated with the welfare state. An old person may not be able to benefit from a home without domiciliary support. A patient discharged from psychiatric care may depend on secure accommodation for adequate treatment to be possible. It has been part of the philosophy of 'community care' that people have to be provided with a package of services if they are to receive the full benefit of each constituent part of the services.

The successful co-ordination of services depends crucially on their relationships at a number of levels. However, such co-ordination depends not so much on the formal structures of the administration as on the level at which the service is operating. Billis (1984), in discussing 'welfare bureaucracies', describes five basic 'strata' or levels of operation of a social service:

5 Comprehensive field coverage
This is the level of policy-making and planning. The concern is to create a framework of services to meet a range of needs. Much is done at central government level; there is also corporate planning in local authorities.

4 Comprehensive service provision
This is the organisation and direction of a complete service, like a housing department, a social services department, a hospital or a social security office. Billis emphasises the broad territorial focus – an area in a range of responses are possible, and in which specific responses are not prescribed.

3 Systematic service provision
This is a responsibility for providing particular aspects of a service, dealing with a range of problems rather than individual cases. Within housing, rents, housing benefit, maintenance, or allocations constitute systems at this level; in other services, it includes officers in charge of residential homes or consultant surgeons.

2 Dealing with problems as situations
This is generally the level at which professionals work; the test is that the professional is able to define the problem and the response. Doctors, social workers, area housing managers and police officers work at this level.

1 Dealing with problems as demands
This is a reactive approach, where service is provided in response to a specific demand; the response made is prescribed for the person who makes it. Receptionists or social security clerical officers are examples.

People within the agencies do not usually work exclusively at one level; some of the work is at one level, some at another. Housing officers may well find that their work stretches across all the levels. A general practitioner may be involved at levels 2 and 3, and sometimes at level 1. A higher executive officer in social security may equally move from level 1 to 3.

The classification of levels here is *not* based on the conventional distinctions between directors, deputy directors and so on, which is a distinction which is based in status rather than types of work. The director of a housing association (probably level 3) may have a lower status than a doctor (level 2); a team leader in social services (level 3) may have a lower status than a doctor (level 2); a team leader in social services (level 3) may have a lower status than an area housing manager (level 2) but an equal or higher status than the co-ordinator of a Citizen's Advice Bureau (possibly level 4). What is really important for practical purposes is not status, but who comes into contact with whom, and in what sort of context. Billis's classification is an attempt to classify different levels of work, based on the range of services and the approaches which different tasks involve; people working at level 4 or level 2 will need to contact each other, irrespective of differences in their status. Researchers and planners, for example, generally work at levels 4 or 5, which means that researchers come into contact with directorates whereas many senior professionals at level 2 do not. Campaigning groups, within the voluntary sector, are also concerned with levels 4 and 5, in contrast to neighbourhood advice or welfare rights centres, who work mainly at levels 2 and 3.

Housing interacts with the other services at each of these levels. At level 5, the level of policy, the main contact tends to be determined by the need to plan the use of resources, though there are other issues, like economic development, which require consideration at this level. To function adequately at this level, housing officers need to have an understanding of the criteria for decision making used by different agencies, the constraints on the organisation, and in particular the financial possibilities and restraints. At level 4, the problems which are resolved within certain defined areas, though some of these areas will cut across conventional service boundaries. The plans made concern service delivery. So, for example, community care plans will initially require contact between a range of providers at level 4, including, for example, a director or deputy director of housing, a district community physician, the director of a Council for Voluntary Service, a social services area director. Here, again, the housing officer needs to understand the criteria which are applied in different agencies, and the constraints, but in addition it will be necessary to understand details of the organisation of different services, the professional structures, and the constraints that this imposes on practice.

The next level, level 3, is the level at which service delivery is organised and controlled in practice. Much of the formal structure of housing departments locates control at this level — a problem when housing officers try to make contact with other services, including social work and health care, which have relatively little emphasis on the organisation of systems, and much more on professional activity at level 2. Effective communication and co-ordination depends on understanding the precise role which the responsible managers have, and the constraints upon them.

Level 2, the level of professional workers, is probably the most significant in everyday practice. Housing officers are likely to come into contact with a bewildering array of workers. They include, for example, general practitioners, hospital doctors, health visitors, district nurses, occupational therapists, social workers, probation officers, community workers, lawyers and welfare rights officers; but there is no universal agreement as to many job titles, tasks and posts, with the result that effective communication can only be established by a gradual process of contact and negotiation. Level

1 is important from the point of view of the consumer, but less so from the point of view of contact between professionals, because the actions workers must take are laid down for them; the nature of the work does not necessarily bring the person doing it into contact with other people in other agencies.

Housing officers working with individuals, at levels 1 and 2, are likely to need a fairly detailed knowledge of the systems in operation. In the first place, they need to be able to refer people to the appropriate places. Secondly, housing officers receive a constant stream of referrals from other agencies, a stream which comes in such volume that many despair of ever identifying priorities within the referrals, and either ignore them completely or look for some system through which priorities will appear automatically. But the referrals are often coming precisely because there has been an expert assessment of the person's need; one has to know where the expertise lies in order to know what the referral means and what weight should be attached to it. In practice, many of the problems of interaction, and much of the experience of practioners, are geared to work at these levels, particularly level 2, where the housing officer is trying, sometimes in tandem and sometimes in competition with other professionals, to assess the needs of a particular person or group of people and to respond accordingly.

Undeniably, the increasing degree of contact between services and professions has led in many cases to friction. The Institute of Housing complained to the Barclay committee on social work (1982) that 'liaison between SSD's (Social Service Departments) and housing departments is too often incorrectly balanced, with junior social workers having to consult more senior housing managers'. This is really a rather silly complaint, being more concerned about seniority than the functions which the officers are performing; a senior probation officer or doctor may well have to consult a housing officer of much lower status. The comment reflects the tension experienced at that time by housing officers seeking to adjust to a new set of roles; the profession has moved on since.

Conflict over administrative and professional roles is not confined to a specific period, or unique to relationships with housing; the same sort of problems which arise between housing, social services, social security and the medical profession arise between social services and the medical profession, and social services and social security. The conflicts are sometimes represented as if they were personal — male versus female, graduate versus non-graduate, senior versus junior professions, professional versus bureaucratic — but this conceals major organisational differences. The differences arise, in part, because the services work within a range of different traditions, and have different priorities. The medical profession is the oldest established, and it has traditionally treated other workers in caring professions as subordinate. It has fiercely preserved its professional discretion in treating patients, but it has done so by emphasising an exclusive personal relationship with patients which often directly obstructs co-operation between agencies. The administration of social security does not claim to be a profession; it is operated within the bureaucratic framework of the civil service. Social workers are expected to identify and respond to risks, which are intangible and often unprovable, and to persuade others to respond to them.

The conflicts reflect, too, organisational constraints. The primary concern of housing officers has been the management of the housing stock, which has shaped the approach of housing management towards the welfare of tenants. The health service has developed around the hospitals, which have fought to resist the shift of resources towards community-based primary care. Social workers have had to balance increasing pressures from growing statutory responsibilities and the expectation that they can produce results with limited, and in some cases with no, resources. Social security services have to deal with an astonishing number of claimants — a local office is likely to have thousands of callers in a week — and rely on a vast administrative machine rather than a personal contact with clients.

It is not really possible, within one book, to give the full flavour of the interactions between the different services; the inter-relationships are too diverse. Even if it were possible, the book would not make very much sense if it was simply to describe the functions of particular professions or services without putting them into their context. To work effectively in co-operation with other professionals, one needs to understand their role, the criteria on which they operate and the constraints under which they work. There is, then, a need to consider services at all levels of operation.

This part considers the structure and organisation of the main social services with which housing services come into contact. It also tries to develop some understanding of the constraints which they operate under, and some of the issues facing the services: issues which, like co-ordination or finance, may reflect or parallel debates in the provision of housing services. The aim is to help to construct a framework, from level 5 down, within which housing officers will be able to organise their knowledge and information about different services and professions. A first step to understanding the issues is an outline of the structures of government through which the services are organised.

Central government

From the point of view of the welfare state, the most important government ministry is probably the Treasury. The Treasury was reformed internally after the Radcliffe Report in 1959. Since then, much of the structure of central government has also been reformed. The highest, administrative, grades of the civil service were reformed after the 1963 Plowden Report. The ministries dealing with social policy were mainly formed in the 1960s:

  1964 Department of Education and Science
  1966 Ministry of Social Security, formed from the Ministry of Pensions and National Insurance and the National Assistance Board.
  1968 Department of Health and Social Security, the first 'super' ministry, bringing together two major departments, the Ministry of Health and the Ministry of Social Security. The DHSS was also responsible for supervision of the personal social services in local

government. During the mid-1970s, the financial systems for health and social security were firmly established as separate, and the breakup of the DHSS into two ministries in 1988 reflects this.

1968 Department of Employment and Productivity, formed from the Ministry of Labour and the Department of Economic Affairs.

1970 Department of the Environment, formed from the Ministry of Housing and Local Government, the Ministry of Public Works, and the Ministry of Transport (which later became independent again).

The reform of services within ministries followed this reorganisation. The Local Authority Social Services Act was passed in 1970; local government was reformed in 1972; the National Health Service was reformed in an Act of 1973. Because the 1972 and 1973 Acts both came into force in January 1974, this was the date of reforms in the administration of education, housing, social services and health. The main aims of these reforms were *managerial efficiency* and — shortly to prove much more important — *economic planning*.

Reforms within departments followed a similar pattern, mainly taking effect after 1974. The effect was to create a system in which the Treasury allocates to departments, and departments to services. Effectively, the Treasury now has full control over spending, except in the case of social security, which is still not subject to effective limits and which is as big as health, personal social services, housing and education put together.

The Treasury is responsible for both the formation of economic policy and the control of public spending. The principal minister controlling public spending is the Chief Secretary of the Treasury, the Chancellor's second in command. Public spending is controlled through a system known as the Public Expenditure Survey Committee, or PESC (though it does not seem now to be a 'committee' in any meaningful sense). The principle of PESC is drawn from the American 'Planned Program Budget System' (PPBS)

Public expenditure in real terms, UK (£m; base year 1984–5)

Function	1980-81	1983-84	1986-87
Housing	7308	4530	3558
Education and science	17099	17132	15955
Health and personal social services	18194	19136	20065
Social security	31086	37908	40365
Defence	14388	16174	16883
Overseas aid etc.	1938	2662	2387
Agriculture etc.	2099	2544	2286
Industry, energy, trade and employment	7440	7052	6037
Arts and libaries	713	761	765
Transport	6115	5559	5306
Environmental services	4974	4938	4266
Law and order	4894	5679	6132
Other spending	3469	2853	7058
Privatisation	-521	-1194	-4329
Total	119,196	125735	126735

which allocates resources by programme rather than by ministry of administrative unit. The process produces a rolling programme of expenditure for each major area of social policy, published annually in *The Government's Expenditure Plans.*

The way these figures are presented is slightly arbitrary. Expenditure on housing, for example, does not include mortgage interest relief to owner-occupiers, and housing benefit has sometimes been considered as social security, sometimes as a housing subsidy (it constitutes part of social security in these figures, but is currently being moved back to the housing budget). The broad figures for 'health and personal social services' disguise a wide range of activities and substantial changes in the patterns of spending. But the figures do provide at least a useful indicator of the direction and priority attached to different programmes.

Local government

The system of local government in England and Wales before 1974 consisted of:
- London, divided after the 1965 London Government Act into 32 boroughs and the City. The Greater London Council had a range of general responsibilities, including housing, transport and planning.
- County boroughs. These were all purpose authorities with a wide range of responsiblities.
- Non-county boroughs. These were divided into County Councils, with responsibility for public health, welfare, and education, and District Councils (Urban or Rural), with responsibility for libraries, parks and housing. In Scotland, the division between counties and parishes fulfilled a not dissimilar role, though the structures and development of Scottish local authorities were very different.

The Redcliffe-Maud report (Cmnd 4040, 1969) criticised the existing system. Services were diffused in too many units. The small size of many authorities made them inefficient. Transport planning was obstructed by the number of authorities involved. And the areas were not based on any rational division. (It is striking, from a contemporary perspective, how far opinion has moved in the opposite direction, with the argument for decentralisation as the basis for a service which is more personal, flexible and responsive to local needs; the Wheatley report, on the reform of Scottish authorities, was perhaps more in tune with current thinking.) Redcliffe-Maud suggested three levels of government:
- 8 provincial (or regional) authorities,
- 81 unitary authorities, with the responsibility for all main services
- a system of local councils to represent, consult and offer some basic amenities.

The minority report to Redcliffe-Maud, by Derek Senior, proved to be more influential. He argued for a two-tier system of local authority, with responsibilities divided between them. This was more politically acceptable to local councillors concerned about their loss of power, and it was what the government opted for in the 1972 Local Government Act. The reform of local government led to a system divided between county councils and district councils. In metropolitan areas, districts provided all main services; in non-metropolitan areas, which accounted for most of the population, counties were responsible for education and social services, and districts for housing. (In Scotland, though the arguments were different, the results proved very similar; the regions fulfill the functions of the English non-metropolitan county.)

Since the foundation of the welfare state, local authorities have lost an enormous amount of power to central government. This includes the responsibility for transport, fire and police (to any significant degree), health services, social security, gas, water, and electricity. They may now be on the point of losing responsibility for the provision of housing, though that remains to be seen.

Central v. local government

Probably the most important control which central government has over local government is that of finance. Local government is now financed in part through rates (shortly to be replaced by a community charge), and partly through the block grant from the government. The Department of the Environment allocates funds to local authorities. Allowances are made on the basis of:

- an assessment of 'reckonable expenditure'. This is basically an assessment of need, and the calculation still refers to a General Needs Index. However, central government is moving away from referring to 'need' directly, partly because they do not want to give local government the opportunity to say that 'the government accepts we have certain needs, but will not provide funds to meet them', and partly because one of the main elements in assessing need in the past has been the level of provision local authorities made — a system which directly rewarded high-spending authorities.
- 'reckonable income', which is mainly the rate poundage a local authority could charge.
- a deduction for local authorities which overspend are penalised.

There is a permitted level of spending, called *Grant related expenditure*. Spending on housing is a part of GRE if the housing account is in deficit.

The effects of these financial arrangements on housing are very visible. The block grant system gives almost complete control over total local authority spending. Although the system of housing subsidies is nominally distinct from this process, the grant to local authorities has become the principal source of finance; the effects of housing subsidies are overriden in the long term by the block grant system. Subsidies have gradually been withdrawn, and they now affect less than half the local authorities. Local authorities have been forced to raise rents, and then have had their income from subsidy reduced, which makes them to put up rents further.

There are a variety of other controls which are available to central government.

Financial. Financial powers include:
- the definition of how local authorities raise money
- the powers of audit – a major fetter on local authority action
- loan sanction – permission to raise money by borrowing.

Legal. The government can:
- direct local authorities, on the basis of powers in specific statutes (e.g. s.1, 1944 Educaton Act, requiring local authorities to offer free secondary education)
- require the submission of schemes for approval (e.g. part III, National Assistance Act 1948, requiring schemes to deal with homeless people, or residential care for the elderly)
- make local authority action depend on central consent (e.g. consent for compulsory purchase orders)
- introduce an inspectorate
- take default powers to act itself
- give people a right of appeal to the Secretary of State (e.g. in planning enquiries)
- alter the powers of local authorities to act (e.g. the provision of school milk). Local authorities are not able to act beyond their defined powers, or 'ultra vires', which is a considerable fetter on innovation or local authority initiative
- create a right of appeal to the courts (e.g. under the legislation for homeless persons. In general, this only happens if no other remedy is available).

Advice. Central government departments use circulars to advise local authorities how to act. Some are fairly influential, e.g., circulars to housing departments on rehousing discharged servicemen, whereas others are not (there have been many circulars to get housing departments to remove residential qualifications on application).

The limits of central government control are, firstly, political. There are limits to what any government dares to do in terms of increasing rents or cutting services, although many of these limits have been tested to destruction by the present government. Secondly, there are practical limits. If central government wished to remove the powers of a local authority, it would have to assume those powers itself. In rare cases, this might be done: for example, the rebellion of Clay Cross councillors, who refused to put up rents after the 1972 Housing Finance Act, led to the establishment of a commissioner appointed by central government in their place. But the commission never succeeded in collecting the extra rents. Third, there are limits to the power of the law. The courts are a cumbersome apparatus of control. Finally, there are problems in managing the machinery of government; it is not possible to change things overnight. When the Local Authority Social Services Act was passed, which was the foundation of Social Services Departments, some councils took two years to put it into practice. A number of councils have still not got to grips with Housing Benefit after six years.

The main government departments dealing with social policy (summary)

CENTRAL GOVERNMENT   *LOCAL GOVERNMENT:*
                              Counties   *Districts*
                              ◀   *Metropolitan districts*   ▶
                              ◀   *London boroughs*   ▶

The Treasury
   Economic policy
   Public expenditure
   Government finance

Department of Health
   Health   Personal social services

Department of Social Security
   Social security

Department of the Enviroment
(DoE: created 1971)
   Local government   Structure   Local plans
   Urban policy   plans
                                                  Housing
                                                  Housing benefit
                                                  Environmental health

Department of Employment
   Employment services
   Youth Training Scheme

Home Office
   Police
   Probation service
   Prisons
   Racial problems and immigration

Department of Education and Science
   (DES: created 1964)
   Higher education   Schools
                              Education welfare
                              Mental handicap
                              (5 to 18)

Scottish Office
Welsh Office
Northern Ireland Office

The role of government: an assessment

The services of the 'welfare state' are not the only means by which welfare
is provided. There are three main sectors besides the public sector:
   - the private sector, services provided on a commercial basis;
   - the voluntary sector, including a wide range of activities from the
     work of large voluntary organisations like the NSPCC or housing
     associations to the activities of individual volunteers; and

  – the informal sector, which includes care by families, friends, and
    communities.

However, government is actively involved not only in the direct provision
of services, but also in the finance, control and planning of services through
the other welfare sectors. Rein (1983) classifies four main kinds of
intervention. Government *regulates* services, establishing the rules under
which they operate: for example, private and voluntary residential homes
have to be licensed by local government. It *mandates* services, or instructs
other agencies to act in particular ways: employers are required to provide
statutory sick pay and maternity pay. It *supports* services, mainly by
providing finance. And it *stimulates* services, often by tax incentives. In
practice, the state adopts many of these roles at the same time. If one
considers the development of housing associations, it owes a great deal to
central and local governement: in particular, funding from the Housing
Corporation, the creation of a charitable framework, and co-operation with
housing, health and social service authorities. Even if welfare services are
diverse, the role of government has been crucial, and in practice, social
services in the United Kingdom are controlled in large part through the
structure of central and local government.

  Social housing, equally, has been organised in Britain principally as a
local government activity; the main exception, the housing association
movement, has been heavily circumscribed both by central and by local
government. As such, housing has been centrally involved in many of the
issues raised by a complex and sometimes intractable organisational
structure. The British system is organised, now, from the top downwards, a
structure which lends itself well to political and financial control, but which
creates other problems. The Central Policy Review Staff (the 'Think Tank',
now abolished) pointed to various deficiencies from the point of view of
central government. Central departments are too remote from the centres
of action. There is confusion about who is responsible for what; and it is
difficult to organise a co-ordinated policy when advice goes from one
department to only a section of local government (CPRS 1977).

  There are also problems from the point of view of service delivery. Two
examples spring to mind. One is the problem of co-ordination of housing
and Social Services departments. Homeless people in 1974 were the
responsibility, under the 1948 National Assistance Act, of the Welfare
Department, usually part of the County authority. Following the reform of
local government in 1974, the new Social Services Departments, which
had just replaced the Welfare Departments, were advised to transfer their
hostels and appropriate personnel to housing departments, which were
part of the District authority. SSDs were required by law to house the
families, but housing departments were not. Housing departments were
advised by central government to rehouse homeless families, but they
could not be forced to. The result was that the legal obligation to rehouse
collapsed, a situation which was not remedied until the 1977 Housing
(Homeless Persons) Act.

  Another example might be the care of old people. Old people may be
housed in sheltered housing (district council or housing association), social

services residential care (county council), private care (often paid for by the Department of Social Security) or geriatric care (under the NHS). This causes problems of liaison and co-ordination; the services have different boundaries, different administrative structures and different criteria for the provision. It also creates difficulties in terms of finance. A transfer between different types of accommodation involves a shift of the financial burden from one authority to another.

Examples of this sort occur throughout the social services; in this book, there are references to similar problems of co-ordination of services for mentally handicapped people and child abuse. The structure of services does matter to the people who receive them.

Chapter 4
Social security

Summary. The social security system was initially built around the idea of national insurance. A range of benefits have been added to make up for the deficiencies of the Beveridge scheme, with an increasing emphasis on means-testing. The result is a system which is baffling, and often inadequate for those most in need. The poverty of the tenants means, however, that housing officers are likely to need a detailed knowledge of the system if they are to make any effective response to their needs.

'Social security' is the name given to financial assistance in a variety of circumstances to maintain people's basic incomes. It is important to housing, in part, because there are now clear overlaps between the services; the administration of Housing Benefit involved a direct transfer of responsibility from the former Department of Health and Social Security. It matters, too, as a major source of housing finance. Social security has to be judged, not simply as a form of income maintenance, but effectively as a major element shaping the way in which people behave in the housing market. An obvious example is the government's proposed attempt to reform the private rented sector. The government have assumed that there will be a substantial rise in rents to so-called 'market' values, though it is a strange market in which suppliers are allowed to dictate what is 'reasonable', without reference to the demand. This can only happen if the government is prepared to inject a major amount of subsidy through the benefits system. But most important is that social security performs a major function in providing a basic standard of living for the tenants of social housing. Any change in the level of provision has a clear effect on the life style of tenants, and such changes directly impinge on the housing services.

The social security system

The social security system is enormously complex, consisting of a wide range of different benefits, often with few rules in common. There are five types of social security benefit.

1. *National Insurance benefits,* mostly set up under the Beveridge scheme. These are benefits paid for by contributions; in practice, eligibility depends mainly on a person's work record. It does not depend on a test of means; people might be entitled to benefits even though they have some other source of income. The main National Insurance benefits are:

Retirement Pension. This is for men over 65, and women over 60. Claimants must have contributed for a number of years to qualify.

Invalidity Benefit. Invalidity Benefit is a long-term sickness benefit, paid after six months of incapacity for work.

Survivor's benefits.

1) Widows' benefits. There are three main benefits. All widows covered by insurance contributions get a lump sum payment of £1000. Widows with children get a Widowed Mothers Allowance; those aged 45-65 get a Widows Pension.

2) Guardian's Allowance. These are for people looking after children whose parents have died.

Unemployment Benefit. This goes to unemployed people for up to one year.

2. *Means-tested benefits.* These are for people on low incomes; entitlement has to be assessed according to the resources which a person has. The most important means-tested benefits are:

Income support. This covers over five million claimants; in all, about seven million people are dependent on it. It began life as National Assistance in 1948. It was renamed Supplementary Benefit in 1966, and Income Support in April 1988. It is basically a benefit for people who are not working and on very low incomes. It acts as a supplement to other benefits. It makes up the difference between income and a set level, which is taken to be a person's 'requirements'. If other income increases, Income Support goes down.

Housing Benefit. This covers costs for rent and rates, and has become almost as important as Income Support. It goes both to Income Support claimants and to others on low incomes, who might be in work. It is based on Rent Rebate, which was introduced in 1972; the present system dates from 1982, and was amended in 1988. It depends in general on both low income and the actual costs of rent or rates; the calculation is horrendously complicated.

Family Credit. This was introduced in 1971 as Family Income Supplement, to help families on low wages. It was chosen in preference to a minimum wage, and can be seen in part as a subsidy to employers who pay low wages. It was renamed in 1988, and worked out on a new principle. Like Housing Benefit, it is based in a complicated calculation; claimants get a maximum benefit when their income is below a certain threshold, but the benefit gets reduced as income increases.

Free prescriptions, NHS benefits, fares to hospital. In general, anyone entitled to Income Support is entitled to these, though there is also a separate means test.

3. *Residual benefits.* Residual benefits are discretionary benefits intended to deal with personal circumstances of hardship, usually on a discretionary basis. The most important are:

The Social Fund. Formerly a part of the Supplementary Benefit scheme, this is a system of discretionary payments and loans for cases where people have difficulty in budgeting, people with urgent needs, and special 'community care' cases including the special needs of elderly people, people discharged from institutions, and 'families under stress'.

The Family Fund. This is a charitable foundation funded by the government and administered by the Rowntree trust, to help families with severely disabled children. The government currently proposes to set up a similar fund for disabled adults.

4. *Non-contributory benefits.* There is no test of contribution or of means, but there may be a test of need. The main benefits are:

Attendance Allowance. Despite the name, which causes some confusion, this is not a benefit for people who are being looked after, or for the people looking after them. It is a benefit for people who need to be looked after, whether or not there is anyone who does so – which is to say, that it is a benefit for people who are very seriously disabled.

Mobility Allowance. This is given to people who are unable to walk, or virtually unable to walk.

Severe Disablement Allowance. This is, again, a confusing name, because it is not confined to people who are very severely disabled, and most people who are severely disabled will not qualify for it. It is a special benefit mainly for disabled people of working age who are unable to work, but who do not qualify for Invalidity Benefit.

Industrial disablement benefits. People who are disabled in an accident at work, or from certain recognised industrial diseases, are compensated under a special scheme.

5. *Universal benefits.* Universal benefits are a special type of non-contributory benefit; they are given without a test of means or of need. The benefits include:

Child Benefit. This is an allowance given for every dependent child.

One parent benefit. This is paid to single parents, as an addition to Child Benefit.

Social security policy

The social security system is in a mess. The system is incomprehensible to many claimants; its own administrators often do not know the rules. The benefits fail to reach many of the people who are entitled to them, and it is widely believed (though disputable) that many of the people who do get benefits shouldn't.

Although many of the problems in practice centre on Income Support and the Social Fund, the core of the system is National Insurance. The other benefits have developed to fill in the gaps left by it, gradually gaining in importance over the years.

Social Security benefits, 1986-1987

	Expenditure (£m)	Recipients ('000's)
National Insurance		
Retirement Pensions	17,776	9,525
Invalidity Benefit	2,617	910
Industrial Disablement	408	175
Widows and industrial death	902	435
Unemployment Benefit	1618	935
Sickness benefits	123	60
Non-contributory benefits		
Non-contributory retirement pension	38	30
War pensions	572	285
Attendance Allowance and Invalid Care Allowance	766	595
Severe Disablement Allowance	260	245
Mobility Allowance	507	450
Child Benefit	4425	12,035
One-parent benefit	148	215
Means-tested benefits		
Supplementary Pensions*	997	1805
Supplementary Allowances*	6267	3030
Family Income Supplement†	158	215
Housing Benefit (rent)	3154	5010

*Now Income Support
†Now Family Credit

[The amounts of money which are being dealt with are so large that they are difficult to imagine. There are nine and a half million pensioners. One penny on the pension would cost £95,250 per week, or £4,953,000 a year. Ten pence on the pension would cost £952,500 per week, or £49,525,000 a year. This should help to put into perspective the occasional government claims that they have saved £2 or £3 million pounds by a certain measure. Savings from special investigation into fraud have yielded, net, less than £20 million a year.

To help make the figures more manageable, it is helpful to use the American 'billion' to mean £1,000 million. Retirement Pension, the biggest benefit, costs £17,776,000,000 every year. This can be taken, for practical purposes, to be £17.8 billion.]

National Insurance

The principle behind National Insurance is that people earn benefits by contributions, paid while they are at work. The advantages of an insurance scheme are:

- People should feel they are entitled to benefits.
⊤ Contributions are a way of raising money for benefits.
- Because people have paid for their benefits, it is supposed to be difficult to abolish the benefits. (This has been disproved by the present government, which has abolished earnings-related supplements which people had paid for.)

The disadvantages are:

- People must work to qualify. This leaves out large numbers of people — unemployed school leavers, women who have been looking after children, chronically sick and disabled people. The insurance system may also distinguish the 'deserving' and the 'undeserving' poor.
- If contributions are set too high people cannot pay them. This may mean benefits are set too low.
- Poor people are less able to afford contributions.

The Beveridge report (Cmd 6404), published in 1942, promised a social security system that would cover every person 'from the cradle to the grave'. The Beveridge scheme is still central to the social security system, but it is very doubtful whether social security could be said to have this basic aim. This is, in large part, because insurance cannot have a truly comprehensive coverage. If it did, it would cease to be 'insurance' in any meaningful sense of the term.

Beveridge based his scheme in six 'principles' of insurance: comprehensiveness, classes of insurance, flat rate benefits, flat rate contributions, adequate benefits, and unified administration. All of these principles have been departed from since.

Comprehensiveness. An insurance scheme cannot be comprehensive. Beveridge himself wrote:

> However comprehensive an insurance scheme, some, through physical infirmity, can never contribute at all and some will fall through the meshes of any insurance (1942, para 23).

The people who are left out tend to be those unable to work — long term unemployed (Beveridge had assumed full employment), school leavers, young mothers, chronically sick and disabled people. Beveridge did not take proper account of the position of women — he assumed they were likely to be dependent on male breadwinners — and failed to anticipate trends in divorce and single parenthood.

A number of benefits which were intended to cover people on a comprehensive basis have now been abolished for reasons of economy. They include Sickness Benefit and Maternity Allowance, which have substantially been replaced by statutory provision by employers, and grants for maternity and death, which have been replaced by payments under the 'Social Fund', a discretionary system which covers only the poorest claimants. Contribution conditions for unemployed people have recently been tightened.

Classes. Beveridge's 'classes' of insurance included pensioners and children, to emphasise comprehensiveness. These were dropped in 1975, though children still receive 'credited' (make-believe) contributions. The special class of contributions for married women is being phased out gradually, from 1977 on.

Flat rate benefits and contributions. Benefits and contributions can be flat-rate or earnings-related. Beveridge felt they must be tied to each other if it was honestly going to be an insurance scheme, and he plontributions created problems for low-paid workers. Following Labour's 1957 pensions plan, the Conservatives introduced a limited degree of earnings-relation in 1959. In 1966, earnings-relation was extended to Unemployment, Widows' and Sickness Benefits, but it was removed from Unemployment and Sickness Benefits in 1983 as an economy measure. Earnings-related contributions have remained.

Adequacy. The scheme introduced in 1948 had lower benefits than Beveridge recommended because, the government said, of free school meals. The Exchequer contribution was very limited — 18% of the cost was met from tax, instead of the 50% recommended by Beveridge. However, the level of benefits which Beveridge recommended would have been inadequate anyway, because the rates he proposed were very low, and because he failed to consider the issue of housing costs, which he thought were too difficult to include.

Unified administration. A national scheme was set up after the Beveridge report. But the inadequacy and poor coverage of the benefits meant that other benefits had to be filled in. Some (notably Housing Benefit) are administered by local authorities.

Means tested benefits

Means tests were one of the main alternatives used to fill in the gaps in the Beveridge scheme. The advantages of means tests are:
- they concentrate resources on those most in need
- they are progressive, and redistribute resources vertically from rich to poor.

The disadvantages are:
- they are complex and difficult to administer
- they create a 'poverty trap'. If benefits are given to people on low incomes, they must be taken away from people whose incomes go up. This leads to the 'poverty trap'. Getting out of poverty, Piachaud writes (1973), is like getting out of a well; if you can't jump up far enough you simply slide back to the bottom again.
- they often fail to reach those in need. The only figures available predate the new names and regulations of the benefits, but in 1981 only 71% of people entitled to Supplementary Benefit got it, and 52% of those entitled to FIS.

The poverty trap

A person on Income Support can earn up to £5 before the income is deducted in full; a couple may earn £10, a single parent £15.

A person claiming benefits while working stands to gain very little through an increase in earnings. The calculation is very complicated, because Housing Benefit and Family Credit are worked out only after tax and national insurance have been deducted, but it works out eventually like this: for each extra £1 earned, a claimant might lose, from April 1988:

27p in tax
 9p in National Insurance
16p in Housing Benefit
44p in Family Credit
_____
96p total

A family earning between perhaps £40 and £140 may be little or no better off for an increase in wages.

In practice, not that many people are affected. There are only a limited number of people on very low wages. Take-up is in any case moderate, and people cannot lose benefits they do not receive in the first place.

Low take-up

There are many reasons given for low take-up. First, there is ignorance. People do not know about the benefits or do not realise they might be entitled. Second, there is complexity: claiming is too difficult. Third, people's circumstances change, and people who think their situation will be different in a short time will not always bother to claim. Fourth, the benefits may be too low. The value of Housing Benefit or Income Support may be marginal, and there is very little advantage to some people in claiming both Family Credit and Housing Benefit. The amount of money might not be worth claiming for the effort involved. Fifth, people may be afraid to claim, for example being afraid of the consequences of asking landlords for evidence of rent or low wages. Lastly, there is stigma. People are ashamed to claim. The usual reasons given for this are degrading treatment by the officers; loss of rights; the history of means-testing; a feeling of being 'labelled'; a dislike of 'charity'; and pride. There is a continuing debate as to how important stigma really is (see Spicker 1984). There is no evidence, by the way, that pensioners feel more stigmatised than others; if anything, the most ashamed seem to be men aged 35-55, who feel they are expected to be independent and self-supporting.

These problems haved led many critics to reject means-testing altogether. But many of the same criticisms could be levelled at benefits which are not means tested, like Unemployment Benefit, and they could account for problems in claiming other services which work on a very different basis, like health care or applications for council housing.

Income Support

Although Income Support disposes of only a limited proportion of all the money spent on social security, it is perhaps the most important benefit, because it guarantees a minimum level of income for many recipients.

There are four basic elements to the Income Support scheme.
1. The scale rates, or 'applicable amounts'. These are supposed to cover all a claimant's normal needs, like food, fuel and clothing, apart from housing costs.
2. Extra weekly payments for people in particular situations, or 'premiums'.
3. Provision for housing costs, mainly mortgage relief for owner-occupiers and allowances for boarders. Rent and general rates are dealt with through the Housing Benefit scheme.
4. Deductions. People can have their benefit reduced for voluntary unemployment or striking; there may also be deductions made to cover past debts.

The basic calculation of Income Support is based on the sum of these elements, minus the claimant's existing income.

The number of people dependent on this basic means-tested benefit — formerly National Assistance, then Supplementary Benefit, and only recently renamed Income Support — has grown steadily over the years.

Recipients of National Assistance and Supplementary Benefit (UK: '000's)

	1951	1961	1971	1981	1985
Pensioners:					
with NI benefits	767	1089	1865	1693	1575
without NI	202	234	114	101	105
Unemployed	66	142	407	1384	2028
Sick/disabled	219	280	321	213	293
Single parents	127	138	285	379	556
Others	81	18	22	85	213
Total recipients	1462	1902	3014	3873	4771

[The recent increases in the numbers of sick and disabled people and single parents are the result of unemployment. A single parent or disabled person who becomes unemployed is best advised to claim under those categories, because unemployed people have lower benefits.]

The National Assistance scheme was established in 1948 as a stopgap to cover people in need until the Insurance scheme adequately covered all the contingencies. It was reformed in 1966. The reason for this reform was that a report called *Financial and other circumstances of retirement pensioners* (Ministry of Pensions, 1966) showed that many pensioners were failing to claim National Assistance. The government's response was to change the name of National Assistance to Supplementary Benefit; to increase benefit levels; to introduce a 'right' to benefit for pensioners; and to run an advertising campaign. Following these changes, nearly half a million more pensioners claimed. Atkinson (1969) attributes most of this increase to the people made eligible by the increase in benefits.

The response of governments to the increasing numbers of claimants has been of two kinds. One has been to try to change other benefits to float people off the safety net. The recent fall in the number of pensioners claiming is because of improved insurance-based pensions. The other response was to reform Supplementary Benefit itself, which is the basis of the change to Income Support.

A review in 1978, under the title *Social Assistance,* tried to adapt Supplementary Benefit to its 'mass role'. The review argued for:

- simplification of the scheme, including fewer rates of benefit, simpler rules for assessment, and the introduction of a short-term scheme
- the creation of a system of regular lump-sum payments, and the confinement of other payments to exceptional circumstances
- the replacement of discretion by rights
- changes in the treatment of housing costs (no major proposals were made, however)
- reviewing the position of married women in the scheme (DHSS 1978).

The 1980 Social Security Act reformed Supplementary Benefit. The Supplementary Benefits Commission was abolished. The idea of a short term scheme was dropped — it would create work, not save it — and the idea of regular lump sum payments was rejected. Instead, the single payments scheme was created, replacing the previous system of discretionary payments by defined rules (and stopping most payments for clothing, the largest ground for claims before 1980). A right of appeal to Social Security Commissioners was established. The position of women remained unchanged until pressure from the European Community forced the government's hand. Before 1983, only the male of a couple could be the 'relevant person' in an 'assessment unit'; since 1983, females can also be relevant.

Following the 'Fowler reviews' of social security, which began in 1984, the government has introduced the Social Security Act 1986, with a flurry of subsequent changes, which have led to a number of reforms:

- Supplementary Benefit has been renamed 'Income Support'
- The rights to single payments introduced in 1980 have been removed, and replaced with the discretionary 'Social Fund'.
- The distinction between short and long term benefits, which particularly affected unemployed families, has been abolished. Instead, premiums are paid to families, single parent, pensioners and disabled people. The main losers are claimants under 25.
- Most young people under 18 are now unable to claim in their own right, a belated change introduced in the 1988 Social Security Act.
- Housing assistance was revised: the extra money given to householders was removed, help with mortgage interest reduced, and no support is now given for water rates.

The Social Fund, which is now effectively a separate benefit, deserves a distinct mention. Under the rules of the fund, people can receive loans or grants. Loans are given principally in cases of crisis, or where people have difficulty in budgeting. Grants cover certain special cases, which include maternity, funerals, community care and families under stress. The amount of money an office is able to expend is limited by a budget, and if the budget runs out, payments cannot be made.

Housing Benefit

Housing Benefit covers the costs from rent and rates. Beveridge failed to consider the problem of housing costs, and his benefits were not adequate to deal with them. The main burden fell as a result on the Supplementary Benefit system. People on Supplementary Benefit are given a minimum level of income inclusive of rent, rates or mortgage interest. Until 1982, rent and rates were given as a part of Supplementary Benefit.

People who were not on Supplementary Benefit received a different kind of help, which was not seen solely as a form of income maintenance. Housing Benefit has grown as part of an attempt to shift housing subsidies from houses to people. The Conservative government in 1972 introduced a Housing Finance Act which trebled rents. Rent rebates were necessary for people to be able to pay the increased rent. Private rents were also increased by the Act, which started to ease controls, and rent allowances for private tenants were introduced in the following year. Rate rebates, which the Labour government had introduced in 1967 as an option for local authorities, became compulsory. The Thatcher government has now removed subsidies to council housing almost completely and the importance of Housing Benefit has grown.

The calculation of Housing Benefit was, and is, complex. Initially, a 'needs allowance' was calculated. This was easier to understand when one appreciated two essential principles. One was that it had nothing to do with needs; the second, that it was not an allowance. (For those who are mathematically inclined, the derivation of the needs allowance was actually the constant $\propto$ in a linear equation of the form $x = \propto - ßy$.) At the needs allowance, one received 60% of rent or rates, and the benefit was gradually increased or reduced if income is above or below the allowance. The amount of the adjustment was decided by a 'taper', based on various fixed percentages.

When the rent and rate rebates were introduced in 1972, the tapers were 17% for rent and 6% for rates if you were above the needs allowance. This meant you lost £2.30 for every £10 you had above the allowance. If you were below it, you gained 25% for rent, and 8% for rates — £3.30 more in benefit for every £10 less than the allowance. These rates were amended many times after, generally being increased for those above the needs allowance so that less benefit was paid to people on higher incomes.

This basic model led to a ludicrously complicated system, with obvious problems:

- people could not work out for themselves if they were likely to be entitled; the 'needs allowance' gave no clear guide at all
- the benefit added a substantial amount to the poverty trap

- there was considerable confusion because someone might be better off on Supplementary Benefit than rent and rate rebate, and it took a complicated calculation to work it out.

There were numerous calls to simplify the benefit, e.g. from the Supplementary Benefits Commission, who were dealing with 400,000 people claiming Supplementary Benefit only to cover their rent (see Cmnd 7725, 1979). The 'simplification' of benefit took place in 1982.

- The job of dealing with many housing costs was transferred from Supplementary Benefit to local authorities. This is why the scheme was called 'unified'. Unfortunately, the local authorities had no staff and resources to deal with the problem, and at first no idea of the amount of work that was being dumped on them. They were rapidly overwhelmed and there were massive delays in the payment of benefit.
- Claimants on Supplementary Benefit were to receive all their rent and rates.
- For other claimants, the tapers were revised. At first, the plan was to replace the four tapers by two — 21% and 7% — which split the difference between the old tapers above and below the allowance. This looks like a convenient simplification, but it would also have cut benefits to everyone — lower additions below the needs allowance, higher subtractions above it. Protests led to the tapers of 25% and 8% below the needs allowance being retained, but the new tapers were introduced above the needs allowance.
- To simplify the scheme further, the government introduced two more tapers for pensioners below the needs allowance — 50% for rent and 20% for rates — and gave pensioners a small addition to the needs allowances.
- Finally, to make sure people on low incomes would not be worse off, Housing Benefit Supplement was introduced to cover people whose incomes would be less than Supplementary Benefit plus rent, who would have been entitled to Supplementary Benefit before the reform. (Housing Benefit Supplement was too difficult to calculate, and few people claimed. It did not survive the 1988 reforms, though at the time of writing there are legal cases disputing whether it should finally be considered to be dead or not.)

The government soon enough decided the scheme was costing too much, and put up the tapers for people above the needs allowance to reduce the benefit they were entitled to.

The 1988 reforms changed the basis of the calculation so that benefits would be reduced from the full allowance, rather than adjusted up or down around a central point. The new system is based on an 'applicable amount' — the term is meaningless, but at least it is not as confusing as 'needs allowance' — which is equivalent to the level of Income Support. Above this amount, benefit is withdrawn at 85p for every extra pound earned 65% for rent, and 20% for rates. This seems incredibly steep, but the 'applicable amount' is based on income after tax, and when this is taken into account HB actually adds up to 54½% to the poverty trap — still very high, but less than might appear. The reforms have also cut back benefits sharply to people receiving HB to cover rates alone, and to people receiving Family Credit.

The problems with the Housing Benefit scheme are:
- hardly anyone understands it
- even when people know the benefit exists, they may not realise they are entitled
- there is, necessarily, a vicious poverty trap.
- Housing Benefit is not very effective in getting money to the poor. Relatively few people, Beckerman and Clark point out (1982), are made poor by high housing costs, and the scheme doesn't effectively get the resources to them. The way Housing Benefit works means that a person on a medium income with a high rent can get more in benefit than someone on a low income with a low rent.
- The scheme is not 'unified': a number of housing requirements are still dealt with by Income Support, including help with mortgages and board and lodging, and other requirements are met by general subsidies to owners. The results are often very inequitable.

The administration of social security

Social security is mainly administered by local offices of the Department of Social Security (DSS). But other functions are held by the Department of Employment (which runs Unemployment Benefit Offices), local authority education offices (which administer school meals, education maintenance allowances and school uniform grants) and, of course, local authority housing or treasurer's departments, which administer Housing Benefit.

The local office of the DSS is divided into two main sections: one deals mainly with National Insurance claims, one with Income Support. For most other benefits, including Family Credit, benefits for disabled people and Child Benefit, the administration is mainly located in national centres; the local office can only forward claims, rather than dealing with them directly. The National Insurance section is divided into short- and long-term sections. The 'short-term' sections deals mainly with sickness, invalidity, and maternity benefits. The 'long-term' section deals with retirement pension, widows benefits, and survivors benefits. The Income Support section is, of course, the section with which housing officers dealing with Housing Benefit are most likely to have contact, but it should not be assumed that all the issues have to do with Income Support; for example, more than three-quarters of pensioners rely on National Insurance, and do not receive Income Support.

Claims in the DSS office are not generally dealt with by individual officers, but by a conveyor belt system or 'stream'. Cases are passed to officers with special functions — from 'callers' (reception) to 'assessment' (calculations and payments), with detours for special functions like 'liable relatives' (checking out maintenance payments) or the 'fraud and abuse' command, which is fairly self-explanatory. A case file could be in any number of places in the stream. Many claimants complain that social security constantly 'loses' files, which is not quite the problem; it is a system which is not designed to *find* files, and finding files takes time. Files are retrieved either by sending a messenger to check at different places in the stream, or by a computer-assisted programme apparently being introduced in social security offices (though I haven't yet seen it in operation) which identifies the location of a file by a 'magic pen' of the type used in libraries and shops. Queries take the case out of the stream, which slows down progress on the case; repeated queries, or appeals, can actually stop any work being done on it.

DSS officers are bureaucrats rather than professionals; as civil servants, they are entitled to remain anonymous. Their task is to operate a huge, complex system as efficiently as possible. Most of the work is done by people working at clerical and executive grades in the civil service, a subject which tends to bring out some hostility in housing officers:

> 'It's the *quality* of the manpower rather than the numbers.'
> 'The DHSS staff are changing all the time and this makes them inefficient.'
> 'Abusive and unreasonable some of these people can be.'
> '... they seem to be adequately staffed — it's the quality of the information they churn out. The staff seem to walk around — you used the term zombie, and they seem to walk around with no apparent concern.' (Quotes from R Walker, 1985)

This impression has to be understood in context. The DSS offices are under enormous strain. The average office deals with hundreds of callers, and several thousand cases every week; housing benefit offices have discovered (with some horror) the volume and pressure of work, and many local authorities have had great difficulty managing even this limited part of the system. It would be naive to suppose that, under this pressure, things do not go wrong extensively; many clients report problems (about 30% of those on Income Support), claims are wrongly calculated (estimates vary from 15–25%; the reform of the system in 1988 may have reduced some scope for error). But the most striking thing about the social security system is not how many cases go wrong, but how many are processed successfully and promptly.

It is perhaps also surprising to discover, in a system designed to operate on uniform principles, how much variation there may be between offices. In cases where officers are required to use their discretion, notably in the allocation of the Social Fund, the differences might be expected; research in *Community Care* shows striking differences.

> Don't go to Jarrow if you want to have a crisis. In September only nine per cent of crisis loan claims were successful, with a paltry average award of £22. You're much better off in neighbouring South Shields, with a 97% crisis loan success rate and an average award of £51 (Craig 1988, iv.).

But there were equally differences under the previous system of single payments, which gave people grants on the basis of formal rights. Walker and Lawton (1988) found that people were more likely to be given single payments when there were more people claiming in person and the pressure of work was low.

Poverty and benefit rates

The social security is not only there to help people who are poor, which would be a residual aim. It also has institutional functions, which apply to everyone in a society. One of these is referred to in the idea of 'social security' itself; the idea that people ought to be able to feel secure. This involves not only being protected against poverty, but being protected against the hardships that are likely to arise through a sudden change in circumstances. If people become sick, or unemployed, they should not, the argument goes, have to lose their possessions or deprive themselves as a result. One sometimes hears the comment that 'people on benefit have cars and television sets', as if this was somehow reprehensible. The question is whether they should be forced to sell their car or television before they can receive benefit. If the intention is to offer security, they should not.

However, social security does clearly play a major part in the relief of poverty. The level of Income Support, which provides a minimum income for over seven million people in Britain, is widely referred to, following Townsend, as the 'state's poverty line'. It is nothing of the sort. The state has no poverty line, and if Income Support was used as one, an increase in benefit rates would have the effect of increasing the number of people defined as poor.

The rates introduced for National Assistance in 1948 were nominally based on Rowntree's surveys, but there are many reasons why the rates of benefit should not be identified too closely with Rowntree's measure of poverty. At the time the benefits were introduced, Beveridge used lower figures than Rowntree; the figures were based on calculations for 1938, and no allowance was made for inflation; and the government made adjustments, because of free school meals, which cut the rates for children. In the time following the introduction of benefits, there continued to be changes. Benefits are increased in line with inflation, but inflation is measured by the general increase in prices, not the items used by Rowntree. No account has been taken of the continued availability or non-availability of 'poverty goods' — second hand items, cheap foodstuffs, etc. There have also been some striking changes as a result of policy. Through the 1970's, benefits for long-term claimants increased by prices or wages, whichever was greater. The structure of allowances, particularly for children, was altered, for simplicity, in 1980, and again in 1988. Effectively, as a result, the rates of Income Support now bear no resemblance at all to any subsistence measure of poverty.

Under the Supplementary Benefit scheme, the basic rates of benefit used to be referred to as 'requirements', a term which suggests that they have something to do with an assessment of need; in Housing Benefit, the calculation was based on a 'needs allowance'. The term 'requirements' has now been removed from the legislation; the rates are referred to as 'applicable amounts' instead. The proposed weekly rates of Income Support for 1989-90, including the standard premiums, are:

	16-17	18-24	25-60	60-80	80+
Single person	20.80	27.40	34.90	46.10	48.60
Couple	41.60	54.80	54.80	71.85	74.30
Couple with children	48.10	61.30	61.30	78.35	–
Single parent	31.20	37.80	45.30	56.50	–

Children:
0-10	11.75
11-15	17.35

The safety net provides benefits below subsistence levels for large numbers of people. Piachaud (1980) shows it to be below the subsistence requirements for children. This is particularly true of adolescents, who have all the needs of adults and more (because of the need for clothing as they grow). Mack and Lansley (1985) suggest that serious deprivations start, for most people, when incomes fall below 150% of the level provided for. And research by the Policy Studies Institute (1984) shows that more than half of all the families with children on the basic benefit were in debt, had had serious anxieties about money while on benefit, and ran out of money most weeks. As the authors of the report point out, this last finding is particularly disturbing. To run out of money in any one week is distressing; to do so most weeks is intolerable.

The money problems of the poor

People with very low incomes are likely to run out of money. Clearly, 'luxuries' are likely to be sacrificed — items like newspapers, outings, entertainment — and 'essentials' protected. But the process is rarely so simple. In the first place, it is easier in the short term to save money on some items than it is on others; it is not difficult to go without an occasional meal in order to be able to afford something else. Poor families commonly do go without food. Equally, items like clothing, which are important purchases for the longer term, are liable to be skimped on. Secondly, some 'luxuries' are difficult to sacrifice. Smoking, which has its highest incidence amongst the lowest social classes, is an extremely expensive habit, but cigarettes contain a powerfully addictive drug. People will go without food to smoke. Thirdly, some bills are easier to pay than others. The quarterly bills favoured by gas and electricity boards cause particular problems. Effective saving, in circumstances where people are running out of money, is impossible. A person who puts aside £6 a week will have £78 at the end of the quarter; but heating bills might easily be nearly double that amount. The budget arrangements offered by fuel agencies — asking for both saving towards future bills, and substantial payments off arrears — can only be met at the expense of some other item (like food or rent). Lastly, people do not always put 'essentials' first. Imagine that you have been on benefit for two years, you have not been able to afford to go out for six months, you have debts of £600, and you get £50 in hand. Would you use the £50 to clear a part of your debts? Or might you be tempted — as I have to admit I certainly would — to blow it on some sort of enjoyment?

Rent arrears offer one of the clearest examples of the consequences of poverty on people. Poverty is not the only cause of rent arrears, but it is a primary cause. The central problem is that benefit rates are not high enough to cover many people's normal weekly expenses. Even if there is a specific allowance for housing requirements, income has to be seen overall; and people may have to choose whether to spend their Housing Benefit on housing, fuel or food. Effectively, poor people have to make a choice from a number of undesirable options. One of these options is not to pay the rent. In referring to 'options', I do not want to imply that poor people will deliberately seek to evade their responsibilities. On the contrary; the problem is that they have several conflicting, irreconcilable responsibilities, which include paying their rent, paying their fuel bills, and being able to feed and clothe their children. If a family falls into debt — and it is often difficult to see how they can avoid falling into debt — they have to balance competing claims from different sources in order to be able to manage at all.

Many councils and housing associations serve notice of seeking possession when a family falls into arrears, and seek to evict tenants who fail to make satisfactory arrangements for repayment. Notice does have an effect, because the claims which tend to be met are likely to be those which threaten the family's security to the greatest extent; where the threat of some sanction for rent arrears is largely removed the effect on arrears can be considerable. But this implies that the debts are incurred elsewhere. The Audit Commission seems to view rent arrears primarily as a function of management practice and the stringency of financial controls; they commend, for example, one district council for their outrageous policy of distraining tenants' property once the tenants are two or three weeks in arrears (1986, p.65), and elsewhere criticise a London borough for being reluctant to evict people in arrears (1984, p.30). The Commission's attitude is punitive: 'where deliberate', they write, 'failure to pay rent for a council house amounts to expropriation of public funds' (1984, p.1). This shows no understanding of the situation poor tenants face. Derek Fox (1982-83) has found that there is no association between the level of arrears in a borough and the number of evictions. It is the poverty of the tenants, rather than the vigour with which the council pursues them, which mainly determines whether or not they will actually pay.

Chapter 5
Health policy

Summary. The direct relationships between housing and health services have diminished, but there are still points of contact which make it important for housing officers to know about health services. The structure of the National Health Service was redesigned for managerial efficiency, planning and co-ordination, but there are still substantial problems, many stemming from the concentration on doctors as independent practitioners within the service. There are important deficiencies in the provision of care for those who are most disadvantaged.

Housing and health

There are many definitions of 'health'. Health is sometimes seen in normative terms, as a level of physical and mental activity which is somehow fixed or ideal; but these definitions are difficult to sustain in practice. Concepts of 'health' vary between cultures, which implies at best that health is a standard of physical and mental well being appropriate to a particular society. Health is often defined as a state of being necessary to perform certain physical and mental activities. This all depends on a wide range of factors, including biological factors, environmental factors, nutrition, and the standard of living. In other words, health can be seen as a function of welfare.

Few of the issues which cause ill health are dealt with directly by 'health services'; they are, rather, issues in the 'welfare state' as a whole. When, in the 19th century, Chadwick identified poor health as a major cause of pauperism, his response was to improve sanitation, not to introduce more extensive medical care. The origins of public housing in Britain were under the auspices of the Ministry of Health. With the improvement in housing conditions of the last thirty years, and the growing body of evidence that ill health is related to class and poverty, it is now probably fair to say that housing is no longer thought of in Britain as a principal element in public health.

The precise nature of the links between housing and health are difficult to establish. There is clearly a great incidence of poor health among people who occupy poorer housing, but the reasons for the connection are not straightforward. One view is, simply, that the bad housing causes the poor health. If a house is damp, it fosters conditions like bronchitis, and will make arthritis worse. A further, related, possibility is that housing will create conditions which foster disease in people who are vulnerable to it. Bad housing leads to stress, and stress makes people vulnerable to illness. Infections spread more rapidly in cases where people are overcrowded. Schorr (1964) suggests that overcrowding is linked with mortality, infant mortality, TB, pneumonia, neurotic stress and depression. Cold housing does not usually cause hypothermia directly (see Wicks, 1978), but if a person who is liable to hypothermia is in a cold house, it may be fatal.

On the other hand, it may be that the people who live in bad housing are also more likely to be ill. If people in lower social classes live in worse housing, and people in lower social classes have worse health (for whatever reasons) then people who live in bad housing will have worse health. The range of explanations which are given about inequalities in health — genetic, environmental, class based and poverty based — apply equally to the range of housing which they occupy. People who are poor have little choice about where they live. They have not only bad housing, but also poor nutrition and a worse education. Their ill health may be the result of a position in society, rather than the direct result of the housing in which they live. At the same time, the importance of housing for health should not be underestimated. There are clearly cases in which housing does directly affect either a person's health, or a person's prospects of recovery.

Over the years, changes in housing policy have reduced the level of contact between social housing and health services, and most of the formal connections between them are residual elements of a previous time. The relevance of health services to housing is, first, instrumental: the professions do come into direct contact; and, with the move to 'community care', health services work closely with personal social services in planning and providing for people's needs. Increasing emphasis has been put in the health service on primary care, and on care in a patient's own home. But there are also important issues of principle. The NHS has represented for many people the cornerstone of the 'welfare state', but it is currently beset with problems. These include issues of organisation, planning, priorities and finance, issues which are relevant to every agency working within the welfare state.

The National Health Service

The aim of the 1946 National Health Service Act was to

> promote the establishment in England and Wales of a comprehensive health service designed to secure improvement in the physical and mental health of the people of England and Wales and the prevention diagnosis and treatment of illness and for that purpose to provide or secure the effective provision of services.

The first part of this would imply much more concern with environmental factors, nutrition and prevention of ill health. The second part more accurately reflects the work of the NHS. 'Health services' are better described as medical services.

The main principles associated with the NHS are:

Universality. The NHS is based on an institutional model of welfare, one which accepts dependency and need as issues which are likely to affect all people at some time. People receive health care as a right. Conventionally, the idea of 'universality' is opposed to selectivity, or selection on the basis of need. But the NHS does in practice select people on the basis of need; 'universality' is taken to represent a principle of a right to health care.

Rights. There is no right to health care on demand, and functions which might be thought of as part of a truly comprehensive service, like regular medical checkups for people who appear to be well, are not generally performed. The principal rights in fact are:

- the right to be registered with a general practitioner. The problem with this is that general practitioners also have a right to refuse to accept someone on their list. In London, in particular, there are major problems of finding a GP.
- the right to be visited. A GP must visit a patient on the list who makes a request.
- the right to be medically examined.

There is no formal right to receive any treatment. This is within the discretion, or 'clinical judgment', of the doctor.

Comprehensiveness. The NHS is held to protect all citizens. This has recently been interpreted to exclude people who are not UK subjects, and patients may be questioned about their nationality. The main problem with comprehensiveness is that access to health services depends on registration with a general practitioner. Homeless people in particular have great difficulty gaining access to primary care, because without an address it is generally impossible to register.

A free service at the point of delivery. The initial idea was that no-one should be deterred from seeking health services by a lack of resources. Charges were first introduced by the Labour government in 1950, leading to the resignation from the government of Aneurin Bevan (the architect of the NHS), Harold Wilson (Prime Minister 1964–70 and 1974–75) and Barbara Castle (Secretary of State for Social Services 1974–76). Charges were nevertheless retained, and not removed by the latter two when in power. They have been substantially increased by the Conservative government since 1979.

Blaxter (1974), in a survey of attitudes, found that means tests for health benefits are viewed differently from other means tests. Free prescriptions are 'health', and acceptable, whereas school meals are 'welfare', and not.

The structure of the NHS

When the NHS was formed, it had a tripartite (three-part) structure.

Hospitals. There were 14 Regional Health Boards governing the hospitals. Individual hospitals, or small groups of them, were governed by Hospital Management Committees. 36 teaching hospitals were effectively independent of this structure; most of these were in London.

Family practitioner services. Family practitioners mainly include GP's, dentists, opticians, and pharmacists. These were governed by Executive Councils.

Community health services. Community health was the responsibility of the local authorities. The Health Department of the local authority would be responsible for health visitors, home nursing, occupational therapy, medical social work, and mental welfare. This department, under the Medical Officer of Health, also governed public health — including noise, food standards, and unfit housing — which is now termed 'environmental health' and is quite separate from the health service.

In 1974, the NHS was reformed into a 'unified' structure, with three main levels of management. The first tier included 14 Regional Health Authorities in England (based on the old RHBs); Scotland and Wales effectively constituted separate RHAs. These were responsible for planning and strategy. The second tier consisted of Area Health Authorities, which were responsible for hospital and community resources in an area. The third tier was of District Management Teams, which dealt with the day-to-day problems.

The main aims of the 1974 reorganisation were:

Planning. The new structure was supposed to assist comprehensive planning and evaluation, as well as the planned deployment of resources. At the time the Act was passed in 1973, it was assumed that this would mean planning for growth; in practice, because of economic problems in 1974 and after, it became planning for scarcity.

Uniform standards. The division of resources within the NHS was governed by a new principle of 'territorial justice'. This issue is returned to below.

Decentralisation and flexibility. The AHA's were given a great deal of autonomy in theory. This was quite inconsistent with planning for uniform standards.

Integration of local services. The supposed aim was to integrate hospital and community care services. Both basic hospital services and primary health care, governed by the Family Practitioner Committee, were to be at Area level. However, environmental health was separated out into local government, and personal social services kept separately. Some functions, including mental welfare and medical social work, were transferred to Social Services Departments.

Co-ordination. The emphasis fell in practice on co-ordination. The boundaries of the AHAs were for the most part the same as the boundaries of the County Councils, which were responsible for Social Services, a principle known as 'coterminosity'. Joint bodies were set up, with special finance to make co-ordination work.

Participation. This was not emphasised explicitly, but it was an important aspect of the reform. The AHAs were composed of one-third DHSS nominees, one-third from the local authorities, and one-third from the professions. At the district level, Community Health councils were set up to act as watchdogs, with rights to secure information and visit facilities.

Efficiency. The Heath government (1970–74) was greatly concerned with managerial efficiency. The reform led to the appointment of many administrators, on the basis that it was cheaper to train an administrator than to train a doctor who then switched to administration. The doctors, however, insisted on being consulted, which meant that many committees were set up to mollify them. They then complained bitterly about the time they were spending in meetings.

One by-product of the 1974 reorganisation was the effective break of most of the links between housing and the health services. Local health departments were broken up, and a number of officials who had had important functions in respect of housing, like the Medical Officer of Health, who became a 'Community Physician', found that their roles were redefined by the new health authorities. Environmental Health Officers were established as a local authority function department quite distinct from the health service (though the traditional links with the Community Physician remained). Their role was greatly affected by the authority for which they worked; some moved into housing departments, some departments of environmental health were combined with housing departments, in some cases housing functions were handed over altogether. EHOs retain important responsibilities for the condition of private housing, and in many places the Environmental Health Department rather than the Housing Department has primary responsibility for many housing functions, including not only clearance and unfitness but also improvement and landlord and tenant relations. Health visitors, who were moved into the health service, became primarily identified as workers in health education, and their role in respect of housing (which had been limited) diminished even further.

The 1982 reorganisation
The 1974 reorganisation led to a great deal of disruption, and was heavily criticised. In 1979 the Royal Commission on the NHS (Cmnd 7615) recommended that no further changes should be made in the near future, because of the difficulties changes would cause. Despite this, the NHS was again reorganised. The government argued in Patients First (DHSS 1979) that there were too many tiers, too many administrators, a failure to take rapid decisions, and money being wasted. In 1982, AHAs were abolished, and smaller District Health Authorities replaced them, largely based on the old districts. (The main exceptions are in Wales and Leicestershire, which have retained former AHA boundaries.) This represented the abandonment of a number of the principles of 1974.

  – *Co-ordination.* The introduction of DHAs threw the idea of coterminosity out of the window. One Social Services department might have to deal with three or more health authorities.

- *Local integration of health services.* The Family Practitioner Committees remained at Area level.
- *Participation.* Local authority representation was substantially removed.
- *Decentralisation.* The basic reason why AHAs were removed, rather than RHAs or District Teams, was that they had become politically inconvenient. Lambeth AHA, most notably, had protested government cuts and refused to operate government policy. The authority was subsequently relieved of its powers.

The aim of efficiency alone was reinforced, though this was not so much through the structural reform as through managerial policies. The subsequent Griffiths report led to the establishment of single managers with substantial authority within the NHS.

Planning the NHS

The Department of Health defines national policies priorities. Strategic planning is undertaken by the Regional Health Authorities. This includes commentaries on key problems and needs, assumptions about resources, outlines of the aims and priorities of each service, and reviews of DHA plans. The District Health Authorities provide the basic information used to form these plans. They make operational plans outlining annual plans for service development, statements about resources, and long-term local strategies. Officially, the DHA is the 'basic planning unit'. In practice, because DHA plans go through the RHA to the Department of Health, and finance comes from the Department of Health via the RHA, they are greatly constrained.

The results of these plans are in theory combined with expected developments in the personal social services (though the planning system for the local authorities seems to have died in its sleep). They are presented in a programme budget which identifies client groups, a principle which directly reflects the pattern of control of public expenditure nationally.

This system was introduced as part of the 1974 reform. The first document, in 1976, was *Priorities for Health and Personal Social Services,* a 'landmark in the history of the National Health Service' (Klein 1977). This identified the main priority groups as being elderly people (because of population increases) and mentally handicapped people (because of previous underfunding). The case was never clearly argued.

The distribution of resources

The policy of the NHS, since reorganisation, has been to redistribute the available resources in keeping with the system of priorities. This reflects, in part, a general desire to economise on health services, though it is important to recognise that the NHS is very cheaply run in comparison to health systems in other developed countries.

The process of redistribution has taken place in two main ways. There has been, first, a major redistribution of resources for health care from hospital care to care in the community, with the inevitable result that hospitals have been closed. This began with the closure of small acute and geriatric hospitals. Subsequently there has been a significant reduction in places for long-stay geriatric patients, and the development of nursing care in the private sector. This has not always led to a reduction in expenditure, because the needs for geriatric care have progressively increased, and because control of expenditure in the private sector is much less effective than control in the public sector. Another significant development, perhaps even more important, has been the discharge of large numbers of mentally ill and mentally handicapped people from long-stay institutions.

Second, there has been an attempt to redistribute resources from richer regions to poorer regions, through the process known in England as RAWP. RAWP stands for the Resource Allocation Working Party, set up in 1975. (Scotland, Wales and Northern Ireland have similar, but separate systems — respectively, SHARE, SCRAW, and PARR.) Finance for hospitals and community health is distributed by RAWP between regions. This makes it possible for Treasury cash limits to be strictly observed.

RAWP works on a formula based principally on the distribution of population and standardised mortality and fertility rates, which are national death and birth rates adjusted for the age and sex of the population in different regions. The figures are then adjusted for any flow of patients between regions.

Objections to RAWP have been of two kinds. The first concerns the method used to distribute resources, which falls between two stools; it is neither simple enough to understand nor complicated enough to represent different needs. There is no significant correlation between mortality rates and sickness, measured by the amount of acute sickness reported to doctors, the amount of absence of work through sickness, or the length of stay in hospital beds. Mortality was selected as the best available indicator of ill health; the problem with morbidity (the incidence of sickness) is that it is more often identified where there is more service.

The second type of objection concerns the principle of 'territorial justice' represented by RAWP. RAWP has led to gradual redistribution from richer regions to poorer ones (though because Scotland and Northern Ireland have been dealt with separately, their position has been protected in relative terms). Consultants in high status hospitals have argued for the protection of 'centres of excellence', rather than equality. The root of this objection, and part of the reason for RAWP's existence in the first place, stems from the concentration of resources in certain locations. London gives the clearest example. When the NHS was formed, there were a large number of high-status hospitals concentrated in the city centre, including e.g. UCH, Guys, Barts, Kings, Westminster, St Thomas's and Charing Cross. For administrative purposes, London was divided so that these hospitals served a large quadrant. However, they continued to swallow a high proportion of resources in their region, and in specific Area Health Authorities, like Lambeth, the centre of the dispute with the government over funding which led to the 1982 reform. Although London was technically better provided than anywhere else, everything apart from the hospitals in the centre was short of funds, and people in Chingford or

Croydon could legitimately object to the absorption of funds by central London. Similar problems occurred in Oxford, because of the university hospitals; Oxford AHA's economies were the subject of considerable controversy (see e.g. British Medical Journal 17.1.81).

When the NHS was reorganised in 1982, some boundaries of District Health Authorities were altered to make it possible to fund high status hospitals within the DHA budget. DHAs were intended to serve a maximum 500,000 people. Leicestershire AHA, serving 800,000 people, was converted directly to a DHA, with the same boundaries; South Notts. was given a catchment area of 600,000 people. Both these DHAs contain university hospitals.

Co-ordination

Co-ordination is intended, according to a 'Think Tank' report (CPRS, 1975)

- to concentrate on specific needs
- to ensure that provisions which depend on other services actually happen
- to increase the effectiveness of services
- to prevent services hampering each other
- to achieve things which one agency alone couldn't
- to get economies of scale (e.g. by sharing resources like laundries).

Co-ordination between health and social services has been promoted in a number of ways. There have been coterminous boundaries (abandoned in 1982), and an elaborate mechanism for joint consultation, which has included Joint Consultative Committees, consultation with local authorities on health plans, Joint Care Planning Teams, and Joint Finance, which has been particularly successful. However, according to Lee and Mills (1982, ch 8), there have been three main problems. Services are not necessarily agreed on priorities. Professional rivalries may interfere with co-ordination. And operational issues, that is, immediate problems, have tended to outweigh strategic (long-term) ones.

The literature on co-ordination has concentrated primarily on the relationship between health and personal social services. Equally, though, much of the work of housing departments is linked with the work of health services: examples include not only the traditional functions of environmental health (like clearance and unfit housing) but also dealing with the specialist needs of old and disabled people, mentally ill and mental handicapped. The contact between housing departments and health authorities tends to be limited, and though housing departments are sometimes now included in formal joint planning procedures, there is no sense in which housing officers are regularly included in the multi-disciplinary health care team. Rather, housing officers faced with health problems tend to take the view that their task is to provide the housing, while others offer 'support'. This is, I think, a deficiency. In the first place, housing is a form of support, and housing officers need to become experts in understanding the impact that housing, location and related facilities have on people's lives. Secondly, housing officers are often first-line contacts with clients, and as such they can perform important functions in monitoring a person's condition or offering advice and support to those in need.

Medical care

Primary care
The core of the NHS is primary care. Although primary care is much wider than the work done by doctors — it includes, for example, optics, dentistry, chiropody, and pharmacy, amongst other specialities — it is largely based, in organisational terms, in general medical practice.

General practice. 70% of the population see their GP once a year. General practitioners treat 96% of all reported illness. GPs are very limited in their capacity to provide medical care; their principal role is diagnosis, prescription of drugs, referral and certification. About two-thirds of consultations are for minor ailments, and 21% for chronic conditions. The main single cause of consultations concerns respiratory ailments (21%) (see Hicks 1976).

Patients have a right to be on a GP's list, but GPs equally have a right to refuse patients. The NHS pays GPs a *capitation* fee, based on the number of patients adjusted for age. There is a minimum list of 1000 patients before practice expenses can be received, and a maximum of 3,500 (4,500 for a partner in a group practice). The average list is 2,100. In some areas, GPs refuse patients because of concentration on private practice, but preserve a minimum list to draw resources from the NHS. This is particularly true in areas of London (notably Kensington and Chelsea). A further problem in London is the number of elderly doctors working in single practices (double the national average). The effect is that, although London on paper is better provided than anywhere else, 10% of the population of London have to rely on hospitals for primary care.

The NHS tries to discourage GPs from setting up in certain areas. If average lists are less than 1,700 patients, the area is 'restricted' and a GP cannot set up. If the number is 1,700–2,100 the area is intermediate and the GP can only buy into existing practices. Areas with averages over 2,500 are 'designated' and incentives given. GPs are not salaried, a direct result of the negotiations for the creation of the NHS, and most run their own practices. However, the NHS pays for practice expenses, including the rent on premises, and since the 'doctor's charter' in 1966 70% of the cost of two employees. The effect of this has been to expand the number of receptionists; the majority of GPs run appointments systems. More than 1 GP in 5 now however works from a health centre, which is run by the NHS.

Effectively, then, when one is dealing with a GP, one is dealing with an independent professional, rather than someone working within a structure of authority under the control of the health service. There are often guidelines on specific issues, but few directives and few common approaches or policies.

This inconsistency leads to one obvious problem in relation to housing — that of the problem of evaluating referrals. If GPs are independent practitioners who have a broad 'clinical freedom' to do as they think fit, it is evidently going to be difficult to apply any uniform standards or criteria. Because some doctors refer on demand — and some even charge patients for writing notes — it is difficult to know what to make of such referrals. The issues are not confined to housing; social security relies extensively on GP assessments for incapacity to work, and the inconsistency between doctors has led in that context to an increasing emphasis on separate assessment by the Department of Social Security's own doctors. Housing, similarly, tends to rely on Community Physicians to filter out medical referrals.

Health visiting and community nursing. Community nurses provide nursing services to people in their own homes. The role of the health visitor has shifted towards that of a health educator, with responsibilities for a range of clients, though health visitors are still qualified midwives, and the traditional emphasis on maternity visiting is still a strong element in the work.

Health visitors and community nurses are employed by the DHA, but deployed through general practices. Although there are many optimistic references within the service to the concept of the 'primary health care team', the organisation is still geared to the doctors. Hill comments:

> the use of the practice as the unit of organisation treats the one member of the team who is not directly in the employment of the DHA, the doctor, as the lynchpin of the system (1980, p.165).

Health visitors and community nurses are relatively unlikely to take independent action to make a referral; they refer back to the team, and so to the doctor, as the source of their authority. Equally, references to them are usually not made directly, but by means of the practices or health centres to which they are attached.

Acute care in hospitals.
Cases for acute hospital treatment are referred to consultants, who are responsible for the supervision of treatment. Consultants are also not salaried by the NHS, but paid set amounts for the consultancy. They can as part of the contract undertake private practice elsewhere. This arrangement was part of the terms for the initial foundation of the NHS — Bevan commented that he had 'stuffed the doctors' mouths with gold'. The privileged position of consultants is not however shared by junior doctors, who work on short-term contracts, receive less money than GPs and often work impossible hours. This was formerly tolerated because of the prospect of consultancy but as opportunities have become more limited has since 1974 been the cause of major disputes.

Until fairly recently, the consultants substantially controlled the throughput of patients. A consultant's status and power depends in part on the number of beds controlled in a hospital and time allocated for operations, and there is a disincentive to treating patients too quickly — if the waiting list disappears, so does the consultant's claim on the beds or the theatre. The length of stay for similar conditions varies enormously: e.g. an average, in different hospitals in Scotland, of between 6 days and 26 days for peptic ulcer, or 3 to 10 days for appendix removal (Abel-Smith, 1976, p. 112).

Lengthening waiting lists have increased pressure for the rational use of resources. In 1986 there were over 830,000 people on waiting lists for operations. The largest number of these were for

general surgery	(180,300),
orthopaedics	(160,500),
ear, nose and throat	(132,200),
gynaecology	(106,600).

(source: CSO 1987, 7.23)

The length of bed stay has fallen, and — largely because of the developing influence of hospital administrators appointed after the 1974 reorganisation — a number of measures have been introduced to improve efficiency, including intensive use of operating theatres, 5-day wards, and beds shared between consultants. But there are still substantial differences between hospital regions, differences not only in cost, but in the pattern of treatment. In Oxford, there is a rapid throughput of patients and intensive use of bed spaces; in Hull, with a much less pressurised use of hospital places, patients are much more likely to be admitted immediately (Laurance 1988).

When a patient is in hospital, the consultant is the person primarily responsible for all aspects of a person's treatment. This is commonly taken by professionals within the hospital structure to mean that the consultant has complete control of the patient's case, that nothing can be done without the consultant's consent, and that discharge depends solely on the consultant's word. This is actually not the legal position, but so many people within the NHS believe it to be true that it has virtually become true in practice, and nothing will be done without reference to the consultant. It can lead to problems. A social worker from the hospital (who is not employed by the NHS, but by the Social Services Department, and who is not accountable to the consultant) may negotiate issues concerning a patient's discharge. During negotiations, it can happen (and does, in some hospitals, disturbingly often) that the patient is discharged summarily without the social worker being informed, on the consultant's order.

Prevention and health

The NHS's commitment to improving the health of the population was for a long time interpreted purely in terms of medical care. Prevention received a low priority, and tended to be confined to such issues as vaccination, school health and post natal care. The importance of cost brought prevention once more to prominence in the 1970s, although it is still only a very limited part of the NHS budget.

There are two main types of prevention. *Primary prevention* implies stopping a person from developing a problem. It can be done, first, by changing the environment, which has been the approach of public health services. Second, it may be possible to change people's behaviour. This is attempted through health education; advertising; legal restrictions, like licensing of pubs; and financial disincentives, like taxation on cigarettes and alcohol. Third, illnesses can be prevented by changing people's condition. Vaccination is the obvious example of this. *Secondary prevention* takes place by identifying a problem in its early stages to prevent its progression. Examples are screening of women for breast and cervical cancer, or advising mothers to have an abortion after amniocentesis identifying that a child may be disabled.

Issues in preventive medicine include, for example,

- Smoking. Smoking is probably the single largest cause of serious ill health in Britain. The major fatal diseases in Britain — cancer and heart disease — are clearly and directly related to smoking, and smoking also makes a substantial contribution to accidents through fire. Smoking is, in addition, an evident cause of major impairment, including respiratory ailments, strokes and circulatory diseases. The government's response has been to combine health education with financial disincentives in the form of high taxation. This has been surprisingly effective; more than eight million adults in Britain have given up since the campaigns started.
- Road accidents. Seat belts and crash helmets have been made compulsory by law. These measures have led to a clear fall in certain types of injury (though there is a controversial argument that there has been a displacement of risk onto other road users).
- Alcohol. Yarrow (a former senior medical officer at the DHSS) estimates that 15%–30% of all male admissions to general medical, orthopaedic and casualty departments in hospitals are heavy or problem drinkers, and argues that alcohol creates even more problems for the health service than smoking (Yarrow 1986). The emphasis has fallen on changing behaviour, with uncertain effect.
- Protection of child health. Perinatal and infant mortality has been a major concern. The arguments for maternity care within hospital have been (on the face of it) to do with prevention; the NHS can better respond in extreme cases if the mother is in hospital. This is arguable: Finland, with one of the lowest perinatal mortality rates in Europe, also has a much higher rate of home births.

Other issues include, e.g., fluoridation of water supplies, nutritional problems, sexually transmitted diseases, drug addiction and AIDS.

Perhaps the most striking omission from this list is housing. Housing was, in former times, one of the most important elements in public health, or, as it is now more often called, 'community medicine'. The reason for its relative decline in importance is not that housing does not have a major effect on people's health, but that for the most part it is no longer directly blamed for the most serious medical conditions from which people may suffer.

Inequalities in health care

The Black Report (DHSS 1980) details major inequalities in access to health care according to social class. Like welfare, health is distributed unequally in our society, and there are clear differences in the incidence of ill health by social class. People in lower social classes, including children, are more likely to suffer from infective and parasitic diseases, pneumonia, poisonings or violence. Adults in lower social classes are more likely, in addition, to suffer from cancer, heart disease and respiratory disease. There are also gender-related problems. Men in lower social classes are more likely to suffer from malignant neoplasms (cancer), accidents, and diseases of the nervous system. Women in lower social classes suffer more from circulatory diseases, and endocrine or metabolic disorders (DHSS 1980). However, despite the poorer health of working class people, the NHS offers more services, of higher quality, to the middle classes. The problem becomes what Tudor Hart once called an 'inverse care law'; that those people in the worst health receive the least services.

The reasons why working class people fail to use the services might be behavioural or cultural. The demand for health care is different from different groups. Working class people are said to be less able to explain complaints to middle-class doctors, less able to demand resources, and more willing to tolerate illness. But the problems might also be simple practical ones. Working-class people are less likely to have access to a telephone, less likely to have cars, and less free to take time off work without losing pay. Doctors' surgeries are more likely to be in salubrious areas, and so difficult to reach.

The Black report argued that 'any inequality in the availability and use of health services in relation to need is in itself socially unjust and requires alleviation'. The report called for a universalist response including:
   – increased priority for children and disabled people
   – more emphasis on health prevention
   – improved information about inequalities
   – more community resources
   – more co-ordination of services
   – a comprehensive benefit for disabled people, and
   – the abolition of child poverty.
Although the policies may well be defensible, the conclusions were almost wholly unrelated to the analysis of problems in the first part of the report, and they were repudiated by the government.

Chapter 6
Personal social services

Summary. The personal social services are concerned with various need groups in a range of settings; they are often identified with social work, but this constitutes only a limited part of the range of their work. The differences between housing and social services arise largely from different professional perspectives and criteria for work with their clients; but there is a substantial overlap between the work of housing agencies and the work of personal social services, to the point where some local authority departments are even being combined.

There is no clear or coherent category of 'personal social services'. They are often identified with Social Services Departments (SSD's; in Scotland, they are Social Work Departments). In Britain, these departments have developed piecemeal, as a residual category of services not provided by other agencies, and both the groups served and services provided read very much as a disconnected list of tasks. The client groups include:
- children who are abused, neglected or without support
- young offenders
- elderly people
- mentally ill people
- mentally handicapped people
- physically disabled people.

The services are provided within particular settings, including area teams of social services departments, residential care, domiciliary care (services provided in the person's own home), day care, and hospitals (and sometimes medical practices). Residential care, domiciliary care and day care constitute by far the bulk of the services provided. Social work, as such, is a minor part of the activity of SSD's. Other settings which are often included within the personal social services are probation, and work with adult offenders (in Scotland, probation is part of Social Work departments); education welfare (in schools); community work; and work undertaken by the voluntary sector. Much work with groups like drug users, single homeless people or women who are victims of marital violence can be considered to be 'personal social service', even though there is no statutory remit to help these groups. Similarly, the voluntary sector sometimes undertakes specialised tasks, like counselling or family therapy, which can otherwise only be a limited part of statutory work.

The work done in Social Services Departments is closely connected with the work done in housing departments. It is clear enough that the client groups being served are often the same. This is particularly true of services for old people, disabled people and mentally ill people; but even in the work which seems to imply less direct contact, like child care and mental handicap, there is a substantial link because of the emphasis in SSD's on work with families. Both departments are concerned with planning resources to meet needs. But the connections go far beyond this. Much of the work of housing and Social Services Departments is similar in kind, notably the provision of domiciliary services, and residential care. To a large extent, the work of social services and housing departments seems to be converging. Social work has become increasingly involved in provision for material needs; social housing is dealing more and more with issues in community care, and the special needs of particular client groups, which are the subject of the third part of this book. There have been moves in some areas to develop closer links between Housing and Social Services Departments, to the point where some departments have even been combined, for example, the department of 'Personal Services' in St. Helen's, created in October 1984, and most recently the combination of services in Bradford. The degree of co-operation looked for is likely to increase.

The development of the personal social services: 1948–1970

After the abolition of the Poor Law in 1948, personal social services were largely the responsibility of three departments. First, there were the *Children's Departments,* responsible for fostering and adoption, child care, group homes, residential nurseries, family casework and assessment and reception centres. The Children's Departments were formed after the Curtis Report (1946), which recommended the establishment of a Children's Officer; the report was partly influenced by the O'Neill case, in which a child was killed by foster parents. The 1948 Children Act made the Children's Department the only department a local authority had to establish by law. The responsible ministry was the Home Office. The powers of Children's Departments were at first very limited. In 1952, following pressure from the Children's Officers, they gained the power to *investigate* cases of neglect; in 1963, following the Ingleby report (Cmnd 1191, 1960) they gained the power to undertake *preventative* action.

Health departments were established as part of the health services. They were responsible, amongst other things, for domestic helps, day nurseries, mother and baby homes, health visitors, occupational therapy, training and occupation centres, Mental Welfare Officers, the register of childminders, Child Guidance, and almoners (hospital social workers). There was a gradual increase in responsibility with the development of community care plans from 1963 onwards.

Welfare departments carried the residual responsibilities which did not conveniently fit into other places. These included residential care for the elderly, homeless families, handicapped registers, holiday schemes, occupation centres, social work support, and registration of homes for the elderly. The welfare departments had the main responsibility for the care of the elderly, and disabled people; in 1962 they gained the power to provide meals, services and recreation.

Seebohm

The Seebohm Committee was set up in 1965 to review the question of establishing a family service. It reported in 1968 (Cmnd 3703) with a recommendation to unify personal social services into one department. Scotland was ahead in this; the Social Work Departments there, which also incorporated work with offenders, were based on the recommendation of the Kilbrandon report (Cmnd 2306, 1964) for a 'social education' department, and were formed after 1968.

The Seebohm Committee's arguments were not detailed. They did not undertake any research because, they said, it would take too much time. The basic case for unification was that it would reduce the number of workers with whom a client had to come into contact. A number of options for unification were considered and rejected:

- the creation of a formal extra co-ordinating body
- a split between a service for families on one side, and pensioners and disabled on the other (because this would have been 'symptom centred')
- a split between children on one side, and health and welfare on the other
- the creation of a special service for social casework
- the unification of health and personal social services. (This is the structure in Northern Ireland and the Irish Republic. It was rejected for Britain because the personal social services would have been the poor relation.)

They argued that *all* related services should come together. So, for example, the new departments were intended to include education welfare and housing welfare (neither of which were actually incorporated after reform).

The 1970 Local Authority Social Services Act implemented the main recommendations. The Children's Departments were transferred intact, despite the resistance of the Home Office which feared it would in consequence become nothing more than a 'law and order' ministry. The Health Departments were broken up in three directions. Some functions, like environmental health, became part of a new local authority department. Some were transferred into the NHS, notably health visitors, and many (though not all) occupational therapists. Medical social work at first went into the NHS but was transferred into Social Services in 1974. Child Guidance went to education, which also successfully resisted any attempts to transfer education welfare.

The Welfare Departments were also transferred, largely intact, to personal social services. Homeless families were transferred to housing by some authorities in 1974, but it was not until the 1977 Housing (Homeless Persons) Act that all housing departments became responsible for homelessness. The role of Social Services departments in dealing with homeless families deserves a brief remark, because it was anomalous; Seebohm considered it quite inappropriate. It led to homeless families being dealt with as if they were somehow in need of social services support, whereas the simple fact was that people were — and are — homeless because they had nowhere to live (see Minns 1972). A similar situation has arisen in recent years with the case of single homeless people, who have to be recognised as 'vulnerable' before they can become priorities for rehousing.

The Seebohm reorganisation met a number of administrative problems. The new departments had to undertake substantially increased responsibilities, for example, because of the 1969 Children and Young Person's Act, and the 1970 Chronically Sick and Disabled Persons Act. The 1970 Act was one of the last Acts of an outgoing government. Some local authorities were reluctant to implement it — the longest took two years. It was closely followed by further reorganisation because of reform (in 1974) of the health service and local government. The Maria Colwell case, of which more later, involved a massive failure of co-ordination, and it can be seen as a basic failure in the aims of the new departments.

The planning of personal social services

Part of the aim in creating the new departments in 1970 was to create a structure that would lend itself to managerial efficiency, a theme which was pursued vigorously by the Heath government (1970-74). The creation of the Department of Health and Social Security in 1968, the foundation of other large ministries, and the reform of the NHS and of local government, were all part of this process. In 1972, social services were asked to produce ten-year plans in accordance with guidelines produced by the DHSS. Authorities were given 'targets' for the level of service to be provided, based on figures which seemed to be drawn out of a hat. The planning procedure was attacked at the time because it lacked any obvious guiding principle, there was no attempt to relate the plans to need, and it asked departments to plan for ten years just before a major reorganisation.

The planning process was incorporated, after the reform of the NHS in 1974, with the NHS planning structure. The reforms were intended to create a structure in which planning would be possible, and to improve co-ordination between services, both by giving social services the same boundaries as health services and by the creation of joint planning bodies. In 1976, *Priorities for health and personal social services* was published (DHSS 1976. See p. 53).

By that time, the purpose of planning had changed. The system was devised at a time of expansion; the economic crisis of 1973-74 meant that it became in practice a mechanism for the restriction of economic expenditure. The policy of both Labour and Conservative governments since that time has been to hold back the growth in expenditure on health and social services, to redistribute resources from the best off areas to the worst off, and to transfer resources from hospital care to community care.

The local authority ten year plans have ceased to play any visible part in the cycle. The allocation of resources is based, not on an assessment of the need for social services, but on the consequences of the NHS planning process, which is based on the programmes put forward by District Health Authorities for different client groups. In this process, social services departments have substantially grown at the expense of the health service. This is not to say that the growth in resources has matched the consequent increase in demand.

The distribution of resources within Social Services Departments

The allocation of resources within Social Services Departments is largely a matter for that department, and there is a wide local variation. In general, however, most resources are devoted to elderly people and to residential and domiciliary care, with only a limited proportion being devoted to 'field social work' as such. The table which follows shows the pattern of expenditure in three authorities. It is drawn from J Black et al, *Social work in context* (1982).

Expenditure in three authorities, 1978-79

	Welsh SSD	Norfolk	Birmingham
Expenditure by type of work			
Residential care	41	45	48
including			
elderly	*26*	*27*	*16*
children	*7*	*12*	*27*
Day care	12	9	9
including			
mental handicap	*4*	*5*	*3*
children	*1*	*2*	*5*
Field work	10	11	12
Domiciliary care	20	21	21
Administration	17	15	10
Expenditure by client group			
elderly	63	62	39
children	12	20	48
mental handicap	11	10	8
younger disabled	11	5	4
mentally ill	4	2	1

Black et al, 1983

Social work

Social work is to some extent defined by the activities of the personal social services and the clienf groups they deal with. What social workers do is interpreted in various ways. The term 'casework' does not refer to one type of activity, but includes many different kinds, such as problem solving (as advisor, broker or advocate); psycho-social therapy; meeting the functional tasks of the agency, that is, providing whatever services the agency happens to provide; changing behaviour; and crisis intervention. The Barclay report on social work (1982) also refers to 'indirect' social work, which includes supervising staff and volunteers, training, management, mediation and community development.

The role of the social worker, and the methods used, depend largely on the interpretation of the problems the social worker is dealing with. Social workers have to assess their client's needs and circumstances, and select a response which is appropriate to bring about the desired effects. Possible responses to problems — this is far from being a complete list — may include some of the following methods:

Personal problems

Psychodynamic approaches
Non-directive counselling
Education
Support
Contract work

Problems with relationships

Family therapy
Groupwork
Contract work (by written agreements)
Work with individuals (as personal)
Conciliation

Problems with the environment

Advice
Welfare rights
Groupwork
Community education
Community work

Holistic approaches

(viewing the problem as a complex of different influences)
Systems approach (identifying key issues within interlocking systems)
Combination of other methods

The kinds of response which are most likely to bring social workers into contact with housing services are, perhaps unsurprisingly, the approaches concerned with the environment, like advice, welfare rights or advocacy work; but the same may happen as a result of some other methods. For example, a social worker seeking to reinforce a client's social skills, an educative process, may give the client some assistance in making an application for rehousing. A worker attempting to influence a family's pattern of behaviour may contract with them to make out a case on their behalf as one part of the bargain. And a worker taking a systems approach — a holistic view which recognises the influence that one aspect of a person's life can have on other issues — may see housing as the key to a different pattern of social behaviour, even though it is the pattern of behaviour and not the housing which is the primary concern.

Social work has been attacked (notably by Brewer and Lait in *Can social work survive?* 1980) as having no specific skills and no clearly defined role. The role of the social worker is ill defined because the social worker has continually to define new roles in relation to highly complex cases. But clearly, the selection and application of appropriate methods is highly skilled, and difficult to achieve with any success. Goldberg and Warburton, in *Ends and means in social work* (1979), found that the types of activity undertaken by social workers in practice are very different between different client groups:

Activity	Child care (% of cases)	Disabled people and pensioners (% of cases)
facilitating problem solving	35	8
information and advice	30	17
assessment	29	20
sustaining	29	8
resources	22	23
advocacy	–	5

The implication here is that work with children is being done at a much higher level. In part, this reflects differences in the types of cases being undertaken, but this is not to say that the skills are not needed as much elsewhere.

The social work profession

The establishment of social work as a profession has been a rapid and unusually self-conscious one. Although there have been social workers and social work training since the turn of the century, social work practice as it is currently understood was not established in Britain until the 1960s. At the time of the Seebohm report, few social workers were trained. The report argued for a *generic* pattern of social work. This was taken to mean that each social worker, as a worker for the whole family unit, should be competent to deal with every part of the family's needs. The Central Council of Education and Training in Social Work was formed in 1971, based on a concept of social work that was generic and all-embracing, including residential care, day care and areas which had previously been specialised (like child care, mental welfare, and work with the handicapped).

However, criticisms of social work have brought the generic model into question, and there has been some dispute as to whether Seebohm might have meant that workers could specialise within generic teams. The current movement has been in two opposing directions.

- *A return to specialisation.* The government has insisted on specialisation in the field of mental health, with the creation of 'approved' social workers. A number of authorities have reorganised services so that particular kinds of work, e.g. with mental handicap, are removed from the remit of field social workers. Others have developed a full set of specialist teams.

   To some extent, this can be said to be happening by default. The emphasis within area teams on child care, and the development of special links with primary health care teams, is leading to a division between services for children on one side, and community care on the other.
- *Community social work.* The Barclay report (1982) sees social work as increasingly, and necessarily, linked to community networks. This means, in part, that social services have to be viewed as a partnership between statutory services and 'the community', including informal and voluntary services. It also implies that social workers have to act to some extent as community workers. (Pinker, in a minority report, attacks the whole idea as trendy waffle. Social workers, he argues, have quite enough to do already.)

   A number of authorities have developed 'patch' systems, decentralising services with the aim of making them more accessible to clients and consumers. This reflects trends in other local authority services, particularly housing, and in some cases the offices are shared.

Alternative approaches to social work

Radical social work. The dominant model of social work in the 1950s was psychodynamic, and the traditional approach to 'casework' was based on the view that it offered a specific response to pathologically based problems. A 'radical' critique was developed in the late 1960s and 1970s, based on a 'structural', principally Marxist, view of the origin of social problems, and a view of social work as an instrument of social control, and in particular of state control (see Bailey and Brake 1975). The strengths of this approach were that it gave a different perspective on a practice that was probably too much concerned with gaining psychological insights and too little with the problems that mattered to clients ('How do you *feel* about your rats?'); and that it focussed attention on alternative methods of working, notably community action, and on the skills required for them. Its weaknesses were that, for one thing, the Marxist analysis is principally concerned with other issues. Marxist texts on social work have reflected at length on social work as state control, but have said little or nothing about key issues such as child abuse. Perhaps more important, many 'radical' texts have been more concerned with political positions than effective techniques. Alinsky (in *Rules for radicals,* 1971) argues that it is rather more radical to get things done.

   Community work. Community work is not necessarily undertaken by social workers; it is carried out sometimes by professionals, sometimes by volunteers, and sometimes within the work of Social Services Departments. 'Community work', though favoured in radical texts, is not intrinsically a politically motivated activity; it is a method which can be used in conjunction with different guiding principles. The term 'community work' covers a range of activities concerned with the way that people relate to each other in geographical areas or large networks of relationships. (A 'community' does not have to be geographical; for example, there is a 'Sikh community'.) There are at least three types of work, though none of them excludes the others:

- community action. This involves an attempt to redress the disadvantages of groups and communities.
- community development. This is concerned to encourage and strengthen the growth of networks of contact within a community.
- community education. The principle objective is to give people within a community the skills to manage their affairs themselves.

Organisation around housing issues is a favoured technique, in part because housing is a major aspect of the disadvantage of certain communities, but also because the improvement of housing conditions is one of the few subjects on which members of a community are likely to have a common interest. It can be difficult to know, in practice, what the primary motive of a community worker is in raising housing issues. If it is community action, the success of a venture is to be judged in large part on its results; if it is community education, the process of collective organisation, through such devices as public meetings or the formation of committees, may be more important.

Welfare rights. Welfare rights, like community work, is not necessarily undertaken by social workers; and, like community work, it may be the work of volunteers or professionals. The professional workers are often appointed within Social Services Departments or some other local authority structure, like Public Protection or Trading Standards.

The welfare rights movement uses techniques derived from law and pressure groups. The principal aims are:

- to protect the rights of individuals as citizens
- to select cases of strategic importance and establish precedents
- to challenge administrative practices and rules, and
- to campaign for improvements in provision.

The greatest success of the welfare rights movement was probably the introduction of legally defined rights to Supplementary Benefit in 1980, which led to considerable expansion of welfare rights work; the greatest failure, the loss of many of those rights in 1988. Welfare rights work is clearly related in its aims to housing aid — in practice, local advice agencies often run both together; the techniques and aims are similar.

Perhaps the most important feature of the welfare rights perspective, from the point of view of housing officers, is the stress on procedural rights. Each individual has the right to have the best case put forward for them, and this is what the welfare rights worker tries to do. This acts as a challenge to the agency, which has to establish that it has acted fairly and appropriately. The primary aim of welfare rights is not to win at all costs — for example, no professional welfare rights worker will knowingly deceive an agency, because to do so would be to put at risk all future cases. It is a way of ensuring that things are being done properly, and if they are not, to seek to change the rules so that they will be done properly in the future.

It is perhaps important to emphasise that the welfare rights approach is relatively rarely adopted by social workers. A welfare rights worker is primarily a negotiator and advocate. A social worker is something quite different, and social workers have other priorities and responsibilities. A social worker who undertakes a welfare rights or housing aid case generally does so with those other priorities in mind.

Housing and social work

Social workers are in a curious position. They are given major responsibilities for the welfare of particular groups, but in practice have few resources with which to produce results. Social work often, as a result, depends on the social worker adopting the role of a 'broker' or negotiator with other services. It would be a mistake, though, to suppose that social workers primarily work as advocates, and a mistake above all to suppose that they act as advocates on demand. They do not; it would be incompatible with their statutory responsbilities for the different client groups.

It is the case, though, that they may be applying different standards and criteria from those applied in housing departments. Housing officers are often concerned with the response to material deprivation; social workers, by contrast, are trained to consider the needs of the whole person, which may include psychological needs, emotional needs, and aspects of their relationships with others. Housing officers tend to be concerned with equity, following clear, consistent standards between people competing for a valuable and scarce resource. Social workers are more likely to be concerned with risk — things which might happen — which may be different, even though the material circumstances are apparently the same. The social worker's perspective is, then, very different from the housing officer's, and this may lead to a basic failure of communication — a failure which is not only unfortunate for the professions concerned, but potentially disastrous for their clients. The report of the inquiry into the death of Tyra Henry, a child in care, comments on what seemed to be at first:

> an unbridgeable gulf between the two departments. Telephone requests for help produced no reaction; letters and memoranda disappeared into a departmental void; any effort on behalf of clients, however urgent, was viewed as token; while individuals who set out to work or cheat the system found it possible to get through. The picture we now have is different, though not much less depressing ... The mental picture we have of the two directorates is of two people attempting to hold a conversation on a dead telephone line. (Sedley et al 1987, pp. 119, 127).

Institutional arrangements tend to rely on the creation of formal mechanisms for liaison, like a liaison officer or team: Waltham Forest, for example, has a Housing Social Work Team, with nominations for 5% of allocations (Hudson 1986). Co-operation does require a willingness to co-operate, and to some extent it may be possible to bridge the gulf between the professions through modifying training programmes, allowing where possible for aspects of joint activity, or sharing offices. If, however, I have been right to argue that the conflicts are to some extent structural, arrangements of this type are not enough. At the level of policy, services will have to agree priorities. This implies joint planning arrangements, and a programme budget — arrangements which have, at least, been successful in furthering co-operation between health and personal social services. Co-ordination at the higher management level calls for an agreed division of labour, commonly defined geographical areas or 'patches', and facilities for joint finance. However, these arrangements do not necessarily overcome obstacles at the operational level. For the practitioners, there is a need for a clear specification of roles and responsibilities, defined procedures, and direct liaison between people with operational responsibility, which implies the participation of interested professionals in a multi-disciplinary team.

Part 3
Community care

Chapter 7
Community care: an overview

Summary. Community care is sometimes described as care in the community, including, for example, care in ordinary housing, or care by the community, which tends to mean care by the family. Residential care is not completely opposed to community care; more and more, it means care where accommodation is provided with varying degrees of support, and housing officers can expect increasingly to become involved in provision of this type.

The idea of 'community care' is a complex one, which is much used in social policy to refer to a wide range of different types of policy. The groups which are considered in this part — old people, physically handicapped, mentally ill, mentally handicapped and children in need — can all be considered, in one way or another, to be the recipients of 'community care'.

The first problem in understanding 'community care' is identifying the nature of the 'community'. Much has been written on this subject, but most of it is of limited relevance to a consideration of welfare services. The 'community' can be seen in many ways: Hillery (1955) lists ninety-four different meanings. The community may be, for example, a group of people with common characteristics, interests or social ties; a geographical unit, like a neighbourhood, in which people live; and a complex network of social contacts between people. Unsurprisingly, with this degree of ambiguity, the idea of 'community care' cannot be a clear one. Bayley (1973) distinguishes care *in* the community — care which takes place within a geographical location where people live — from care *by* the community — care provided in the context of a network of social relationships. However, even within this distinction there is considerable room for uncertainty.

Care in the community

Care that is not in an institution
If the 'community' is nothing more than a geographical unit, then a person

who lives in a particular area is 'living in the community', even if that person has no social contact with anyone in that area. 'Community care' has often not been 'care' at all. Over the past twenty five years, people have been encouraged to 'remain' in the community, which means they are not offered the option of institutional provision, or, in the case of mental institutions, they have been discharged into the community without adequate support. Many of these have been re-admitted into the institutions; the policy of the 'open door' has been described as a 'revolving door'. Current practice has altered in two main ways. Firstly, the principle affecting people in mental institutions now is that 'nobody should be discharged from hospital without a practical individual care plan jointly devised by all concerned' (HC Social Services Committee 1985). Secondly, many of the institutions patients might have been re-admitted to will be closed.

Care in ordinary housing
Community care has come to mean, more generally, care in one's own home. The House of Commons Select Committee report (1985) identifies 'the community' as 'ordinary housing', which seems to exclude many hostels and group homes. The emphasis falls on domiciliary services. Help can be given with self-care (through for example aids and adaptations in the home, occupational therapy, or community nursing) and housework (through the provision of meals, home helps or laundry services). But domiciliary services are desperately under-developed, and it can be very costly to provide services to people in their own homes equivalent to those that they might have received in institutions.

Normalisation
Much weight is given to the idea of 'independence'. However, to participate fully in society, people who have been very dependent need facilities and education. For example, Adult Training Centres for mentally handicapped people emphasise social skills, work or household management. The difficulty here is that 'independence' may expose vulnerable groups to pressures which they cannot cope with.

Care by the community

Care by the members of a neighbourhood
'The notion of a community', according to the Seebohm report, 'implies the existence of a network of reciprocal social relationships, which among other things ensure mutual aid and give those who experience it a sense of well-being' (Cmnd 3703, 1968, p. 147). In practice, 'mutual aid' is very limited, and this seems rather too rosy a view. The problem is often to get even the necessary minimum of social acceptance for people who are discharged from institutions.

Care by community services
The strongest identification of 'community care' has been with the work

undertaken by Social Services Departments, to the extent that the Griffiths report on community care (1988) has argued for a formal concentration of community care within that service. But the term is wider than that: community care is increasingly interpreted in terms of a package of services. 'Community services' include the full range of statutory and voluntary services — including social security, education, health, housing and social work — which are available to the members of a community. There are two main problems in over-reliance on community services. The first, and most obvious, is that the pace of discharge from institutions has exceeded the ability of community services to cope (HC Select Committee 1985). Second, and perhaps more fundamental, these services are mainly designed to help the general public; they are not really geared to very high levels of dependency. The special needs of certain groups often stretch them beyond their capacity. A DHSS report argues that good community care is liable to be costly: 'in some cases the community alternative might only appear cheap because its level of provision could be considered inadequate' (DHSS 1981). A substantial burden has fallen by default on the informal carers.

Care by the family
The main supportive network in the community is the family. 'When the word "community" is used', Wilson writes (1982), '... it should be read as "family". Furthermore, for "family" we should read "women".' More women now stay at home to care for elderly or disabled relatives than look after young children. Pascall comments that there is a tendency for state services to assume that if there is a woman in the family, there is no need or responsibility for intervention in any of the tasks which the woman will be expected to perform: 'it seems that only if there is no woman relative available will the full resources of the "Welfare State" be brought to bear' (1986, p.95). The process is slightly more subtle than this implies. What seems to happen is that social services decide how much support is given after consideration of the household structure — but in practice, within larger and younger households, it is still the women who have to provide the support (Arber et al 1988).

The commitment of families and the level of support provided is often far beyond what the state is prepared to offer. But there are substantial difficulties both for people in need and those who look after them. From the point of view of the person cared for, the family may be part of the problem; it can be difficult to gain independence or to exercise any choice. For the carers, the physical and emotional burden may be greater than they can bear. The main gainer is the state, which is relieved of many of the costs and responsibilities of care.

Residential and community care

Residential care has been seen, traditionally, as a type of care diametrically opposed to community care, and residential institutions have been as distinct communities in themselves, set apart from the rest of society. The picture is a misleading one. The Wagner report (1988) identifies many different types of residential care:

- long term care. This is the most commonly recognised pattern, including many old people's homes, children's homes, and so on.
- respite care. These homes give carers a break.
- assessment. A number of homes, particularly for children, are designed as temporary stages, during which a person's needs can be assessed and a suitable placement found.
- rehabilitation. Some homes, like probation hostels or hostels for former psychiatric patients, are concerned with enabling someone to return to the community.
- therapy or treatment. Examples are hostels for people with drug dependencies, and some hostels for mentally ill people.
- training. There are homes and hostels of this type, e.g., for mentally handicapped people, mothers with young children.
- convalescence, e.g. nursing homes for the elderly or for some psychiatric patients.
- crisis or emergencies.
- shared care or flexible care, arrangements which are increasingly being made for elderly or physically disabled people (Wagner 1988, p.166).

These roles are clearly complementary to community care; and the report comes to the conclusion that, in practice, there is no clear distinction to make between the different forms of care. Residential care should be seen, not as care that is different in kind from other types of provision, but as a pattern of care provided with accommodation. It is a form of 'supported housing'. The report includes, as a result, examples like sheltered housing, group living or core and cluster homes, as forms of 'residential care', and argues that 'housing and social services will need to agree and administer jointly policies for the allocation of supported housing' (Wagner 1988, p.24). This implies a major role for housing services.

MIND, in evidence to the Wagner committee, argued:

> The emphasis is on the provision of ordinary housing accommodation with support put into the house as appropriate. The essential feature of this support is to ensure that people are able to maintain their accommodation, whilst also developing links and relationships within the surrounding community. The intention is that residents become as integrated as possible, taking full advantage of all the services and facilities that are available to "ordinary" people alongside whom they will be living. This after all is true "community care" (cited in Wagner, 1988, p.16)

The committee found this persuasive; I do, too. If the concept of 'community care' has any value, it rests in the ideas of enabling people to participate as members of a community; and people are enabled, not by being left to their own devices, but when they are given the choices, opportunities and means to act which are otherwise denied to them.

The role of housing services

Perhaps the most important concept to come out of the debates on community care is the idea of the 'care plan', or 'package' of services which each individual receives. The elements of community care cannot meaningfully be separated from each other; health, housing, personal social services, and social security have to be seen as inter-related, with the success of each dependent on the performance of the others.

The Griffiths report on Community Care (1988) argued that 'the responsibility of public housing authorities should be limited to arranging and sometimes financing and managing the "bricks and mortar" of housing needed for community care purposes'. It is the Social Services Department, the report argues, which should be responsible for the provision of the human aspects of the services which provide for community care. This view is one with which some housing officers may feel a basic sympathy. They feel that they should provide housing while some other service offers 'support' to people in the community — frail elderly people, discharged psychiatric patients, young people discharged from care, and so forth. The reaction is an understandable one; housing officers do not, in general, have the expertise, knowledge or skills to deal with many of these highly specialised needs. But it fails to appreciate the role of housing in social terms.

Firstly, housing is central to those needs. Housing is not simply a matter of bricks and mortar; it represents the way in which a person lives. Housing can affect the pattern of a person's social relationships; there are those who would argue (like Newman [1973] or Alice Coleman [1985]) that it has a direct causal effect. If family relationships are central to community care, then housing equally plays a part; families live in housing, and problems such as location, overcrowding, insecurity, lack of privacy or noise can have a crucial effect on those relationships. A housing officer needs to know whether the housing is suitable for the person, whether it might have a detrimental effect on the person's circumstances, and whether better housing may have a positive effect. The housing officer needs to be involved in the individual case from the outset in order to maximise the benefit a person will have from the service. To achieve this, housing officers have to act as part of a multi-disciplinary team.

Secondly, a person's home is the basic unit on which the provision of community care depends. Housing officers are often 'primary contacts', officials who have to come into regular contact with people in need. They have access to information that others do not have. They have legitimate grounds for visiting the home, without stigmatising the client. They can monitor; in some cases, they can offer emotional support. If housing officers withdraw from this contact, assuming that someone else will do it, a vital opportunity is lost. It was recognition of the importance of this role which has led MIND, in some group homes for mentally ill people, to arrange for voluntary workers to act *as if* they were housing officers, collecting rent and checking repairs, because this provides a stable basis from which other functions can be fulfilled.

Lastly, the management of property cannot be separated from the issues of dealing with people. Griffiths argued that

> Social services authorities should be responsible for arranging the provision of social, personal and domestic services in sheltered housing, and the finance for those services should be provided through social services, not housing budgets.... I do not intend this to prevent arrangements being agreed between housing authorities and social services departments, for example for the provision of wardens who carry out both property management and personal care responsibilities. Similar considerations in principle apply to alarm systems; the decision whether an alarm system would be an efficient means of meeting an individual's needs should be for the social services authority, which should also be responsible for financing those parts of a system that are not the landlord's fixtures and fittings (1988, p.15).

The basic proposition seems to be supported by the Wagner report, which accepted the distinction between 'accommodation' and 'support' (1988, p.17), and argues that wardens should be 'first line representatives of social services' (1988, p.20). But Wagner's approach was based on a model of service in which housing agencies and social services would work closely together, jointly planning and providing essential services. Griffiths, by contrast, seems initially to have based his argument on a strict division of labour, which misunderstood what sheltered housing is, and what housing officers actually do. Elizabeth Anson, the chair of the Association of District Councils' housing committee, argued:

> You cannot divorce the physical and social aspects of housing. The narrow concentration on bricks and mortar by national and local government in the 50s and 60s is a mistake for which we are now paying dearly. It would make no sense to remove housing welfare workers and wardens from housing authorities or housing associations. This would create a new organisational boundary to cross (in *Social Services Insight* 1988).

Griffiths, to his credit, subsequently retracted. The important issue, he recognised, is not necessarily the question of which service provides care, but who should have the responsibility for ensuring that services are provided where those services are not available. This leaves much greater scope for Social Services to work with housing associations and housing departments; and housing authorities might, in certain cases, act as agents in certain cases for the social services authority (*Inside Housing,* 18th November 1988, p.3). This is a significant move in the direction of the Wagner report; it is based in the desire to bring about co-ordinated planning and service provision, with defined responsibilities. It builds on, and anticipates, trends in the field; the moves in some local authorities towards closer liaison, and even unification, of housing and social services is an important recognition of the importance of a cohesive system of community services.

Chapter 8
Elderly people

Summary. Old people are a diverse group, but there are a number of commonly found problems. They include poverty, ill health, disability, social problems and poor housing. Housing agencies can make a major contribution to the welfare of elderly people both in co-operation with other services, and in their own right.

There are over 8 million people over the age of 65 in the UK. This has little significance as a fact in itself; there is no intrinsic reason why people who are over 65 should present special problems for social services. There is a widespread image of old people as being people with failing faculties, finding difficulties in coping, and becoming dependent on others. It is true, of course, that many old people are likely to become dependent, and it is important for a range of services to be available for old people with special needs. On the other hand, the idea that old people are likely to become dependent is often translated into a norm — an expectation that they ought to be dependent, coupled with social pressure to make sure that they will be. Walker (1980) refers to the problem of the 'social construction' of old age, a set of ideas and attitudes which act to limit the ability of old people to participate in society. This pressure shows itself both in small and in large ways. The small ways are linked with the way people react to old people: the assumption that, if an old person mishears, they are becoming deaf; if they forget or fail to understand, their brain is failing; that if they are in ill health, it is something they should expect as part of old age. In a broader social context, there is an expectation that people will stop working at 65, or even sooner. When pensions were first introduced, they were for people over 70. The current age of retirement is 65 for a man, 60 for a woman. A man who retires at 65 has a life expectancy of 77; a woman retiring at 60 has a life expectancy of 81. Early retirement is increasing, and men over 60 who are unemployed are no longer required to be available for work. This is a relatively recent phenomenon. Twenty years ago, about a quarter of all men did not retire at 65. It is now less than 7%. But this expectation of dependency is almost in inverse proportion to the abilities of the population involved. In many ways, the outlook for elderly people is improving substantially; the life experience of people aged 65 now (born in 1923) is massively different from people born twenty years before, with an experience of considerably better nutrition, health, education, housing and financial situations.

Poverty and social security

Many pensioners are deprived. They often live in old housing; those in private rented housing are particularly likely to live in bad conditions. Their savings have been eroded by inflation. They are less likely to possess certain items, like fridges and washing machines, which have become part of the modern household. Old people on Income Support are particularly at risk of hypothermia. [It should be noted, though, that this is mainly because of very old age, poor nutrition and failing health, *not* because of lack of heating: see Wicks 1978].

Poverty is, for some, the result of an extended period on low incomes. It is difficult to say how far old people can be considered 'poor' because they are lacking certain material resources, like central heating, wall to wall carpets or refrigerators; a person who has never had these things may well take the view that they are not necessary. Old people in general are less likely to be poor than younger families on similar incomes because they are more likely to have a stock of resources — and it is worth noting that unemployed people receive substantially less on benefit than pensioners do, both because pensioners receive a premium on the basic rates, and because unemployed people are more likely to have dependent children, for whom the benefit rates are particularly inadequate. But clearly, if an old person was poor throughout her lifetime, she is more likely to be poor now. For some, poverty is simply a continuation of previous circumstances.

Financial provision
There are well over nine million people receiving some form of pension on account of age. Nearly all of these have National Insurance pensions, but in many cases the National Insurance is not enough to provide a basic minimum income. 18% of claimants, about 1.7 million, receive Income Support/Supplementary Benefit, and it is estimated that another 0.8 million are eligible but not claiming. Those who do receive National Insurance tend to be on the 'margins' of poverty, often just above the Income Support level.

The basic aim of pension schemes is to provide elderly people with an adequate income in retirement, though how much is 'adequate' is very much open to dispute. The first state pensions introduced in Britain, under the 1908 scheme, were universal and non-contributory. They were also found to be very expensive, which meant that when further social benefits were introduced — health and unemployment benefits, in 1911 — there had to be some sort of contribution to pay for the system. Non-contributory pensions were largely removed in 1925, and pensions have been contributory since then.

The main purpose of contributions, as this suggests, is to raise money to pay for the pensions. There are two main types of pension schemes. There are those which are *funded,* which means that the money is saved (put into a fund) and invested. Most private schemes are like this. The central problem of funded schemes is that they cannot easily cope with inflation; the money which they have is constantly being devalued. So, instead of relying on a fund, there are other schemes which work on the principle of 'pay as you go'. The money in a 'pay as you go' scheme is not saved, but used as it comes in; contributions now pay for benefits now. This is the model of state pensions in Britain. The so-called 'National Insurance Fund' does not exist; it is an accounting fiction (or, if you prefer, a fraud on the public: all the money has gone).

The Beveridge report (Cmd 6404, 1942) proposed a funded scheme, maturing over 20 years, with flat-rate benefits and contributions and a 50% exchequer contribution. In the 1946 National Insurance Act, the Government introduced a 'pay as you go' scheme. They set up the 'National Insurance Fund' but were only prepared to make an 18% contribution to it. This meant that benefits were kept low and contributions high. A number of plans were subsequently put for reform, though it took twenty years before major reforms took place. One relatively minor reform was the introduction of graduated pensions in 1959. The graduated pension was based on a flat rate contribution and benefit, with a small earnings related supplement, although people could 'contract out' of the earnings related element to take an occupational pension instead. Although many pensioners now receive some graduated pension, the benefit from it is very limited. The largest change came with the 1975 Social Security Pensions Act. It introduced earnings related contributions giving a flat rate benefit, a form of concealed tax, with an earnings related supplement ('SERPS', or the State Earnings Related Pensions Scheme). The government's commitment was far from generous. The exchequer contribution was limited to 18%, and the scheme was based on pay-as-you-go with 20 years maturity. New Society (1969) commented, about a previous pensions scheme which included this proposal, that the effect of phasing in a pay-as-you-go scheme over 20 years is that we promise ourselves pensions paid for by our children but aren't prepared to pay for our parents now.

The other important elements of the 1975 scheme were, first, that the value of contributions was to be inflation proofed before retirement. Second, there would be equal rights for women, obtained in part through protection for home responsibilities, and in part because the level of pension would be based on the best 20 years of a person's working life. Third, there was a complete protection for occupational pensions, which would be guaranteed inflation proofed by the state. This greatly favoured the development of private schemes, and realistically the pensioners who are currently best provided for are those with an occupational pension.

Although the amounts paid by private pensions are often small, they play a crucial part in lifting people above a minimum income. (One side-effect has been that pension funds have become the largest single bloc of investors in the stock market.)

With SERPS and occupational pensions, the pensions of people retiring now have been gradually improving. However, the increasing expense — pensions are the largest single element of the social security budget, and comparable in size to expenditure on defence or health services — meant that this was unlikely to continue. In 1985, the Conservative government proposed to abolish SERPS, and to replace it by private schemes. They estimated that by 2035 there will be only three workers for every two pensioners. 'It would be an abdication of responsibility to hand down obligations to our children which we believe they cannot fulfil' (Cmnd. 9517, 1985). They have now passed legislation to cut the level of pensions which SERPS will provide in the long term, but not yet. In the meantime, they have altered the rules to base pensions on 40 years of working life — which will reduce the rights of women to pensions — and have encouraged people to contract out of the state scheme.

The effect of earnings-related pensions on pensioner poverty is likely to be substantial. There has already been a major shift in the composition of households in the lowest income brackets. Only ten years ago, it would have been true to say that most poor people were old (see Layard et al 1977); now, the elderly constitute only about a quarter of the poorest households (see CSO 1987), and the number is diminishing.

Health and disability

Sickness. The health of old people is often poor. This is not simply because of old age, but also because the diet, housing, occupation and lifestyle of most people in the early twentieth century was not conducive to good health. On average, a person over the age of 75 costs the health service nearly seven times as much as a person of working age. There is some reason to believe this will not be true for people retiring in twenty years' time; the generation raised during the second world war, at a time of strict food rationing, had a far superior diet to their predecessors, and the post-war period was followed by a considerable improvement in basic living standards. One of the main reservations to be made about this optimistic view is that it was also a generation in which the majority of adults smoked.

Physical disability. At least a third of people over 75, probably more, can be classified as 'disabled' (according to DHSS research). In part, this is linked to poor health, and some improvement in the level of disability might be looked for in the future. However, the most common cause of disability is arthritis, affecting at least a million people, and it is far from certain that the situation in respect of arthritis will improve in the near future.

Mental impairment. Dementia (now frequently called 'brain failure') is believed to affect over 4% of the elderly (a figure cited in Slater and Roth, 1977, though the surveys on which these figures are based are very unreliable; they were based on a fairly limited sample of people in one area in 1960). It is characterised initially by gradual loss of short term memory, and followed by a progressive deterioration of long term memory. A person's short term memory is essential to absorb new information; as it deteriorates, the person is less and less able to adjust to changes. A common observation on rehousing elderly people is that in some cases they seem to become rapidly confused. Although this might have happened by coincidence, the process is not usually rapid. What has happened is that they have been able to cope quite adequately in an unchanging environment, with everything in its place and without any events to alter the pattern. When removed from that environment, their inability to cope becomes visible in a way it was not before.

There are two alternative views of dementia. One is the medical view, that dementia stems from a failure of the brain as a physical organ, and so that dementia can only be stemmed by organic change (e.g. through drug therapy). The other is social, that dementia follows when people do not have any reason to use their faculties of memory over a long period of time. Residential workers with the elderly are increasingly using methods of 'reality orientation' to avoid confusion: large signs with the date, time and information about what is happening.

In general, the older a person is, the more likely these problems are to occur. It is possible, in looking forward to the position of old people in the next twenty years or more, that the improvement in health of people aged 65 will simply be offset by larger numbers surviving to 75 and 85, who will suffer from problems which are equally serious.

Social problems

Old people are equally likely to suffer some social problems, often as a direct consequence of disability or failing health.

Isolation. Townsend refers to poverty, in part, as the ability to participate in society. Old people are less likely to be able to participate, not only because of lack of income, but for other reasons. If their faculties are failing, this will present an obstacle to maintaining contact with other people. A person who is unable to move around effectively cannot visit people. One of the effects of deafness is that people are less able effectively to take part in a conversation. The onset of deafness is gradual, and much of it can be simply prevented; but the onset of deafness is so gradual that people are rarely aware that they are becoming deaf until it is too late.

Part of the reason for isolation, too, is that social circumstances change. Friends die, families move away. There are substantial emotional problems when spouses die, not only of isolation, but of bereavement and loss.

The problems of carers. Many old people are looked after by women who are themselves ageing (there are in fact more women at home looking after elderly and disabled relatives than there are looking after children). Caring for elderly people means, in many cases, monitoring their condition, preparing meals, cleaning, and providing company and security. This is not necessarily a great burden, but there are likely to be difficulties in coping with even this amount of dependency. In the first place, the person who is doing the caring — usually the woman in the family — has little opportunity for respite or escape. Secondly, the old person is usually a parent, who has for much of the carer's life been in a dominant position. It is difficult for an old person to adjust to becoming dependent, and often it is more difficult still to become dependent on someone who used to be subordinate to them.

As problems of ill health, disability and mental deterioration increase, the task of carers becomes more and more difficult. It is difficult to live with someone who is seriously demented, and unable to remember a conversation of the previous minute. Sleep disturbance is the most common problem, and some people suffer full 'day-night reversal', sleeping during the daytime but being fully active through the night. Incontinence, even when reasonably under control, is a particularly difficult issue when it requires someone to clean up after their father or mother; although most carers can cope with urinary incontinence, faecal incontinence is too much for many (Sanford 1978).

To a large extent, provision by informal carers, both family and friends, is crucial to provision by the social services, which is often designed to supplement informal care, and, it is commented by feminist critics, assumed to be unnecessary if there is a female who can be expected to provide support.

Personal social services

The basic aim of social services for elderly people is that they should be able to live independently in the community for as long as possible. This is generally associated with the idea of 'community care', though independence does not cease to be important at the point where a person ceases to live 'in the community'; in every setting, including residential or institutional care, independence is important for self-respect and personal dignity. 'Independence' is not a simple concept; there is a wide range of conditions which reduce a person's ability to function independently in society, and in consequence there has to be a range of services available to respond to individual needs. Social care involves, as a result, a wide range of facilities and services which are necessary to support individuals.

A range of responses are available to Social Services Departments. They include, first, domiciliary services, like meals on wheels, home helps, laundry, aids and adaptations in the home. There is social support, e.g. in lunch clubs or day centres. There may be support for carers, including some relief through domiciliary services, respite through day centres or temporary residential care. Lastly, there is a wide range of residential care provision, not all of it under the aegis of the Social Services Department.

Residential care

The main types of residential care for old people include Social Services accommodation, long-stay hospitals, and private nursing homes. These measures provide different degrees and kinds of care, and they can be used most effectively only when the role of each is understood in relation to the others.

Long stay hospital wards are placed either in geriatric hospitals or, increasingly, in general hospitals. The common problems are physical incapacity, confusion and institutionalisation. People are not necessarily in hospital because it is the best form of care for them, but they have been admitted following a crisis, and it proves impossible to discharge them afterwards. Hospitals are geared mainly to medical care; old people who only need nursing are seen as 'blocking' beds required for others.

Part III accommodation is provided, under the 1948 National Assistance Act, by Social Services departments. People need to be admitted to residential care where they are unable, even with services at home, to maintain a degree of independence. However, they should not be so seriously impaired as to need constant medical or nursing care. The way in which this need is interpreted varies considerably; meals are provided, and some personal care, but the homes are not primarily equipped for nursing. Although the homes will usually provide support for residents whose condition is deteriorating, this usually means that they are limited in their ability to take more people who are very dependent. Part III homes often refuse to admit old people who are immobile, or incontinent.

Nursing care is limited. The NHS has only a bare handful of nursing homes itself, though the number is increasing; Part III often does not meet the needs of people who are seriously dependent. The gap has to be filled by the private sector, with the substantial fees being met by the social security system once the resident's capital is exhausted.

Admission to long-term residential care may depend on a number of factors. They reflect, in large part, the person's capacities. Many people in residential care suffer from severe physical handicap, impaired vision or hearing, or mental confusion; they are often isolated and unable to cope on their own. The average age on admission is 83. Many basic services could be provided at home; the crucial point is probably passed when a person is unable to make a cup of tea (Thompson 1973). But admission depends as much on social as on physical problems. Poverty and bad housing may play an important role in the person's ability to cope with their circumstances (Sinclair 1988, pp 260-261). Residential care may be necessary if there is no adequate support — because, for example, there is no family, or because the range of domiciliary services is limited (ibid, pp. 259, 261-2), or because carers cannot cope. But many residents have been admitted simply because there was nowhere else available. There may be 'an awful lot of other very independent residents who either should not have been admitted in the first place or afterwards should have been found accommodation more suited to their needs' (Booth & Berry 1984).

Three models of residential care
Warehousing. Some residential care for old people is simply somewhere to put them. A common image is, Goldberg and Connolly comment, of 'very old people dozing or staring into space in identical chairs placed around the

walls of a large lounge, lining up for toileting and bathing, being dressed by hurried night staff early in the morning and then waiting more than an hour for breakfast' (1983). This picture is repeated throughout the institutional sector.

Horticulture. The term 'horticulture', like the term 'warehousing', comes from the work of Miller and Gwynne (1972). An alternative, positive approach to residential care can be based in the belief that the purpose of a home should be to provide an environment in which the potential of residents should be developed fully. This clearly applies to mentally ill or handicapped people who are being prepared for society, but it is just as relevant to the elderly. The attempt to make residential care like a 'hotel' has been accused of creating dependency: though the guests in a hotel have some choice as to service, they cannot choose the decoration or furniture in their rooms, use the rooms as they wish, or decide freely when to have meals. But the view that residential care should be like a 'home' can also be criticised. Meteyard (1985) argues that a modern, purpose built institution for old people is far better equipped to meet the practical needs of the residents. He calls, amongst other things, for clear signposting, strong lighting, and Tannoy systems.

Normalisation. Normalisation means that people should be integrated into society, while they are in care, to the greatest degree possible. One option is high-dependency housing linked with Social Services, generally known as 'category 2' because it falls between *category 2* sheltered housing and *part* III. Another is group living, where the residents live in small domestic units, and they are encouraged to do as much for themselves and each other as they can. The case for normalisation is partly that people are capable of being more independent than conventional arrangements often allow. Partly, too, it is a recognition that residents have rights, which implies, among other things, that they should be asked what they want. 'The primary aim', a DHSS memorandum notes (1973), 'is to create an atmosphere in which residents can ... live as normally as possible and in which their individuality, independence and personal dignity are respected.'

The basic implication of a policy of normalisation is that residential accommodation should, as far as possible, be seen as accommodation with support — the position argued by the Wagner report. In this respect, sheltered housing has been a very successful alternative to the traditional forms of residential care. However, this success needs to be examined in some detail. 'Part of the case for sheltered housing', Purkis and Hodson argue,

> addresses an exaggerated set of special needs rather than problems whose best resolution may in many cases be good quality, small, ordinary houses, and a wider range of support services linked to them (1982, p.82).

The services which are provided are of uncertain value. There is little evidence to suggest that the formal function of the warden — to intervene in the event of an emergency — is a useful one (see Goldberg & Connolly 1983). Old people who have fallen are often not able to summon help, either because they cannot reach the communication cord (a problem which some agencies have tried to deal with by getting residents to carry communicators round their necks) or because they are not conscious. What is important about the function, however, is not how effective it is, but how effective people think it is. The presence of the warden — the belief that the warden can do something — offers a sense of security. Alarm systems, at first blush, serve much the same purpose.

In practice, wardens may be valued, not so much for the strictly limited emergency cover they are supposed to provide, as for other functions they perform which they are not expected to do by their employers. Some wardens will help residents with shopping, or get in touch with people for them. Some help residents to take their drugs. Some act as a sort of community worker, organising activities and outings. These are valuable functions, but because wardens are not trained for them — and not paid for them — it is by no means certain that they will be ready or willing to fulfil them. The argument of the Griffiths and Wagner reports for the transfer of responsibility for community care to Social Services departments, is probably strongest in this context. Housing agencies clearly need to reconsider the role and functions of warden systems.

Housing

Old people often live in older housing, because they have lived in the same place for a long time. This has implications both for the condition of the property and its tenure. The condition of property is likely to be poor simply because housing does deteriorate with age, but the issue is more complex than that; many younger people in older housing will not suffer from poor conditions to the same extent. Deterioration in older housing often reflects a pattern of maintenance over a long period of time. Many old people are not physically able to do the work required for maintenance. Many are women, from a period when women were expected not to undertake 'men's work', and they lack the skills to do it. And, because the income of old people is limited, they are often unable to raise the finance necessary for work to be paid for. Owner-occupiers in receipt of benefits would have to take out loans against their house to cover any repairs which cost more than a minimum amount. This is difficult for old people to do, because they cannot pay off a loan in the short term, and in the long term mortgagors are reluctant to lend money against a property which may be tied up for many years and which can only be recovered from the mortgagee's estate.

The pattern of tenure among old people is very different from that of the population at large. Among owner-occupiers, elderly owners are more likely to own outright than to be paying a mortgage. This is because incomes are limited, because it is difficult for people to obtain mortgages above a certain age, and because those who had mortgages have paid them off. Secondly, the proportion of people buying their houses has steadily risen since the end of the first world war. Those who never bought lived in rented accommodation, either council or private rented, and it has been difficult for them to move into ownership. As time has gone on, fewer and fewer people have rented. This means, logically, that there is a higher proportion of older people in rented housing.

In the case of private renting, old people are in a special position which is unrepresentative of private renting in general. The reasons for this are mainly historical. The traditional private rented sector, which dominated the housing market before 1914, consisted of houses which were let to tenants on a long-term basis. As owner-occupation grew, the private rented sector went into decline. During the 1920s and 1930s, there were several developments. Owner-occupation grew rapidly; it was possible to buy a house as cheaply as to rent it. During this period, council housing also grew from almost nothing; two million council homes were built before 1939. The effect was to remove a large part of the market for stable, long term rents. After the second world war, the private rented sector was already becoming old — the vast majority of it had been built before 1914 — and it was private rented housing which bore the brunt of clearance policies. The costs of maintenance soared; the income a landlord could gain from rent was limited, not so much because there were controls on rent as because the richest prospective tenants had bought their houses instead. Because owner-occupiers bid up the value of property, the rates of return which landlords could get fell. The basic incentive to landlords now is to rely on an increase in the capital value of the property, which means that they are concerned to sell, not to let long term. When houses are rented out, they are likely to be let in multiple occupation, which increases the rental income a landlord can expect. The houses occupied by old people, by contrast, are those on long-standing lets. It follows from this that the conditions which old people in private rented housing face are substantially worse than in any other tenure, and on the whole they are likely to be worse off than other private tenants. Any private rented house let for the very long term is likely to be old, poorly maintained and probably substandard.

Social housing
Social housing is a relatively recent historical development, and old people in social housing are not usually the descendants of parents who were themselves council tenants, though, as time goes on, this is changing. Old people have usually come at some point into council housing from the private sector. In the past, the main routes were either through clearance or through rehousing from the waiting list. Both routes were possible, but it depended on the area in which one was living; some areas had too many houses in poor condition to allow clearance of every old house, and some local authorities did not take the condition of the house into account when assessing priority for rehousing. (Many still do not.) The third way is to be rehoused as an elderly person, either into council accommodation or into housing association property, which has become much more important in the course of the last ten years.

The growth in the numbers of old people, the range of problems which they are likely to face, and the need to increase the range of options for social care and for satisfactory housing, all point to an increasing role for housing services in dealing with the elderly. But it would be misleading to suggest that the elderly should be treated as a particular group with common needs. Elderly people are a diverse population, and although they may be affected in particular ways by certain types of policy — for example, the deregulation of many controlled tenancies in the 1970s, or the introduction and subsequent abolition of Housing Benefit Supplement — these cannot be seen as policies directed specifically at elderly people. To a large extent, housing provision for elderly people can be considered on the same terms as housing for anyone else.

Chapter 9
Disability

Summary. The problems of disabled people are diverse, but there are some important common elements. The majority of disabled people are elderly, and yet many of the services available do not provide for elderly people at all. The problems of low income and bad housing are probably more important and appropriate as a response to the needs of disabled people than aids or adaptations which assume a common set of physical problems.

The problems of disabled people are very diverse. They include conditions like blindness, inability to walk, deafness, inability to sustain a physical effort, epilepsy, and chronic illness; the definition of disability can be extended to include mental illness and handicap or alcoholism. Stopford (1987) outlines nine principal categories:
- neurological disorders (disorders of the nervous system). These include, for example, cerebral palsy, multiple sclerosis and stroke.
- neuro-muscular disorders, e.g. muscular dystrophy and poliomyelitis
- communication disorders, e.g. autism
- metabolic disorders, e.g. cystic fibrosis or diabetes
- blood disorders, e.g. haemophilia and leukaemia
- bone disorders, e.g. arthritis or brittle bone disease
- chest and heart disorders, e.g. asthma, heart disease
- skin disorders, e.g. eczema, psoriasis; and
- sensory handicaps, e.g. hearing or visual impairments.

This is far from being a complete list. [Stopford's book, *Understanding disability*, is a valuable reference point for people in the caring professions without medical expertise; it explains what is known about over forty different disorders, the principal symptoms, how the disability is likely to affect family living, employment, education and mobility, and details of relevant support agencies.]

A DHSS survey published in 1971 estimated that there were 3 million adults disabled in Britain. This survey was mainly concerned with physical capacity — the ability to move one's limbs and use one's organs — which is a very limited definition. Townsend (1979, pp. 686-688) suggested the number of disabled people might be nearer 7 million. The difference between the figures is based not so much on the question of accuracy as of definition. Townsend outlined five basic definitions:

1. An 'anatomical, physiological or psychological abnormality or loss'. This is the definition mainly used to assess disability for industrial injuries, for example, or war pensions.
2. A 'chronic clinical condition'. This includes people with conditions like bronchitis, emphysema and epilepsy, but might not include someone who had lost a hand.
3. A 'functional limitation of ordinary activity'. This is a social definition; it might include, for example, ability to walk or to work. Disability is judged not by what the cause of the problem is, but by the effect it has on a person's capacities. This is probably the most important definition for the purposes of housing, because housing is directly related to one's ability to undertake ordinary activities.
4. A 'pattern of behaviour'; two people with identical physical problems can react quite differently to the same physical problem.
5. Townsend argues that disability is a 'class', or economic grouping; the main thing that disabled people have in common is that they are likely to be poor because of the way their personal limitations affect their lives.

Most recently, a new OPCS survey in 1988 has shown some 6 million disabled people (this was reported prior to formal publication in *Community Care,* 15.9.88).

The treatment of disability as if it was a single problem may mean that disabled people receive insufficient or inappropriate assistance. One of the first things to appreciate is that *most disabled people in Britain are old.* Not only are elderly people overall in the majority — there are four out of six million in the new OPCS survey — but they are vastly in the majority when the most serious disabilities are focussed on (DHSS, 1971). Relatively few chronically sick or disabled people are under 50. Despite this, provision for the disabled is often concentrated on *young* disabled people, or at least people of working age. Of the principal social security benefits for disabled people, only Attendance Allowance is available to the elderly; Mobility Allowance, Severe Disablement Allowance, and Invalidity Benefit are restricted by age. Sheltered workshops and employment quotas have little relevance to most disabled people, as do special schools. The same is true in the voluntary sector; a criticism of the Royal National Institute for the Blind is that it has concentrated on young blind people, who were the majority of blind people at the turn of the century, rather than the old people who constitute the majority of blind people now.

The most important specialised provisions tend, in practice, to be those without arbitrary restrictions on age — housing, health care, day centres, and facilities (like telephones and home adaptations) provided under the Chronically Sick and Disabled Persons Act 1970.

Health and functional capacity

Disability is often interpreted as a 'health' problem. To some extent, it is; many illnesses are disabling, and in some cases conditions which might otherwise be disabling can be cured through medical intervention. Equally, it is true that many cannot be — the inadequacy of medical care in treating back pain, arthritis and many respiratory ailments are illustrative.

There is a tendency to rely on medical evidence as 'proof' that a person is disabled. But functional problems are often more important than medical ones. Doctors are not necessarily equipped to make an adequate assessment of a person's functional capacity; the assessment of a social worker or occupational therapist may be far more relevant.

The assessment of functional capacity.
There are a number of scales used to measure a person's ability to perform certain tasks. In *Measuring disability,* an early pilot study (1973), Sally Sainsbury identifies a number of activities which disabled people may have difficulty with. They included:

1. doing heavy housework
2. doing the shopping
3. preparing and cooking a meal
4. going up and down stairs
5. running to catch a bus
6. cutting toenails
7. washing or bathing
8. hanging out washing
9. tying a knot in a piece of string.

These activities were pointed with 1 point for difficulty, and 2 points if unable to complete the task. This yields an overall score out of 18.

This scheme was intended as a focus for discussion. It seems at first sight very unsophisticated — it is strange to rate people who cannot run to catch a bus with the same weight as people who cannot wash or bathe themselves — but it is much more complicated than it appears. What Sainsbury was trying to do was to rate people according to their *functional* problems rather than their physical abilities. The tasks she concentrates on provide simple tests, but the problems which they cover are not simple ones. If a person cannot tie a knot in a piece of string, it is an indicator of physical problems, like that person's ability to turn a tap on, peel potatoes, sew, or many other activities which involve manipulative ability, depending on fine motor capacity in the hands. Running to catch a bus, which at first may seem an odd inclusion, is a test not only of mobility but also of the person's ability to make a sudden effort. Cutting toenails includes both manipulation and ability to bend. These items are included in the index with some very complex activities, like 'preparing and cooking a meal'. If a person cannot bend, for example, that person will have at least some difficulty with heavy housework, cutting toenails, bathing, and hanging out washing. Effectively, the scale is based, not on a simple weighting of one or two points, but on a balance between different types of disability according to the problems they cause. Sainsbury identified a number of core abilities, which included concentration, co-ordination, sustained effort, manipulation, mobility, reach, and sudden effort. The nine tasks in the points schedule were selected to make an assessment of these factors with an appropriate weight between them.

The scale does have important limitations. The scale is mainly geared to identify particular types of physical disability, leading to problems in applying it to other circumstances. Some of the categories are fairly loosely framed. The selection of the nine topics is based on what they reveal about a person's overall capacities, but many of the topics, like doing the shopping, or going up and down stairs, are dependent on the conditions the person lives in, not just the disability itself. And 18 points does not allow for fine discrimination between people with different types of disability. As a preliminary, pioneering attempt, though, it is fairly impressive.

Scales like this are widely used. An example is the Crichton Royal behavioural rating scale, which is increasingly being used to assess the circumstances of disabled elderly people in residential care (see Goldberg & Connolly 1983). This relies on a fairly basic pointing of factors, including mobility, memory, orientation, communication, co-operation, restlessness, dressing, feeding, bathing, and continence. Items are rated 0 to 3 or 0 to 4; for example

Mobility	0 Fully ambulant using stairs
	1 Usually independent
	2 Walks with supervision
	3 Walks with aids or under careful supervision
	4 Bedfast or chairfast

Co-operation	0 Actively co-operative
	1 Passively co-operative or occasionally unco-operative
	2 Requires frequent encouragement or persuasion
	3 Rejects assistance, shows independent ill-directed activity
	4 Completely resistive or withdrawn.

This scale is, like Sainsbury's, simple to administer. It is inferior to Sainsbury's in three respects. In the first place, the classification is very much more subject to interpretation by the assessor. Secondly, it contains some items which are contentious — particularly co-operation, in which a person is rated on the basis of the difficulties they present to the agency rather than the needs they have as individuals. Thirdly, and most important, there is no clear justification for the balance of points given in specific conditions.

Poverty and social security

Disabled people are also likely to be poor. This happens, in the first place, because people who are poor are more likely to be in ill health. The reasons for the association are disputed (see ch. 4), but it may mean that disability may be seen as a consequence of poverty as well as a cause of it. Secondly, disability interrupts a person's earning capacity. In *The causes of poverty* (1977), Layard et al found that some half of the families where the man was disabled were on low incomes. There is, then, a need for employment, though its importance, relative to the numbers and characteristics of the disabled population, should not be overestimated. There are several main provisions made for disabled people, established by the 1944 Disabled Persons (Employment) Act. One is the quota for large employers, who are expected to have at least 3% of their employees disabled. Virtually no employer meets this criterion, and although it may be possible, under a wide definition of disability, to consider that 3% of the workforce might be classified as disabled, it is uncertain whether they should be. Another is sheltered workshops for disabled people. There is also the Disablement Resettlement Officer in the Department of Employment. The DRO maintains a register of disabled persons (quite separate from the registers kept by Social Services Departments, which is one reason why people usually cannot accurately say whether they are registered disabled).

The third, and most obvious, reason why disabled people are poor is that they are likely to be old, and old people have limited incomes.

Benefits
The only main benefits available until the 1960s were legal action for personal injury, the Industrial Injuries scheme (1896/1946), the contributory Sickness Benefit (1946), and War Pensions (1917). Pressure for improvement came from three sources: the Disablement Income Group, at first a one-woman pressure group; the thalidomide case, which attracted considerable interest in the Press over an extended period; and research showing the extent of disability.

1970 Attendance Allowance. This was the first general allowance available to people on the grounds of severe disability. Despite the name, it is not an allowance for people looking after others, or even for people who are actually being looked after. Rather, it is for people who *need* to be looked after — a condition which is used effectively as a test of the most severe disabilities. The basic rules are that a person should need, by day, 'frequent or constant attention in connection with their bodily needs' or by night, 'prolonged or repeated attention'. There is a lower age limit (2 years), but no upper age limit.

1971 Invalidity Benefit. This was a long-term sickness benefit, based on contributions while working. It floated many recipients above the level of income when they would need to claim Income Support.

1975 Mobility Allowance. After campaigns by the Tricycle Action Group, the Sharpe report (1974) recommended the phasing out of invalid tricycles, which were unpopular and widely seen as dangerous, in favour of adapted cars, which were cheaper, but which could be used by three times as many disabled people. The government was not prepared to finance cars for disability, believing that the cars would mainly benefit 'helpful' relatives rather than the disabled people themselves. Instead, they came up with the idea of Mobility Allowance, which is for people who are virtually unable to walk. Mobility Allowance was not well received by pressure groups. Alf Morris. the minister, said 'I don't know what they want'. They wanted cars. Motability, a government sponsored 'charity', was set up for people to lease a car with their Mobility Allowance. The advantage of using a charity is that it doesn't have to explain its use of discretion in the way that a government agency does.

Mobility Allowance was at first limited to people under 55; it was later extended to those under 65, but still excludes the majority of people who cannot walk on the grounds of age alone. It is restrictive in other ways; the handicap has to have an organic basis, which means that many people who are mentally handicapped cannot receive the benefit.

1975 Non-contributory invalidity pension. This was available to people who did not qualify for Invalidity Benefit. It was only for people of working age and was not available to married women. In 1977, HNCIP was introduced: the 'H' stands for housewives. There was a test of a woman's ability to perform normal household duties. However, too many women claimed and the rules were changed in 1978 to restrict claims further. Pressure from the European Community to remove sexual discrimination from benefits led to the replacement of these benefits by Severe Disablement Allowance. Claimants who have not been transferred from other benefits generally need to be 80% disabled. The rules have recently been challenged in the European Court on the basis that the discrimination has been perpetuated because of the transfer of people who initially drew their entitlement from a discriminatory benefit.

1976 Invalid Care Allowance. This is a very restricted benefit for people of working age looking after someone who receives Attendance Allowance for 35 hours a week during the day. It has not been available in the past to married women, but this was successfully challenged in the European courts in 1985.

Benefits for disabled people are complex, in part, because they are given on a number of principles. First, there is compensation for disability. Industrial disablement or action in the courts assume that people should be paid if something unpleasant happens to them. This does not extend to those who simply become ill or to those born with disabilities. Second, there is insurance. This is the principle behind Invalidity Benefit. Third, there are payments for special needs. Mobility Allowance covers a supposed extra income need for transport. Supplementary Benefit awarded an extra 30p for every bath over one per week needed for medical reasons, a provision abolished in April 1988; under the Income Support scheme, disabled people now receive flat-rate premiums to cover their extra needs. Fourth, there is desert. War pensioners are the obvious example. Lastly, there is low income. Many disabled people on low incomes rely on Income Support, like others who are poor.

Any attempt to reform benefits is likely, as a result, to conflict with one principle or another. The Disability Alliance argues for a universal Disability Allowance for all disabled people. The advantages of this scheme are:

– it will treat people more equitably
– it should offer a basic minimum
– it will be simpler than the present system.

The disadvantages are:
- it will be very costly
- many disabled people, like war pensioners, have privileges they would not want to see eroded by a more rational system
- not all disabled people are in financial need
- it will separate out disabled people, as the 'deserving poor', from others who are 'undeserving'. This would be undesirable for the social security system as a whole.

Personal social services

The role of personal social services in dealing with disability is, as with elderly people, to maintain independence to the greatest degree. The responses available include, as before, domiciliary services, social support, support for carers and residential care. There may also be training in certain skills in day centres (sometimes restricted to those under 65). Specialist social work tasks may include, for example, dealing with adjustment to disability because disabled people may have problems of self-esteem, or may experience social rejection; and the teaching of specific skills necessary to overcome elements of disability (including e.g. communication skills).

The Chronically Sick and Disabled Persons Act 1970 created a broad range of responsibilities which fell in the main on the new social services departments. The responsibilities included:
> s.1. A duty to obtain information about disability within an area
> s.2. A duty to provide, as required,
>> – assistance in the home
>> – radio, tv or library facilities
>> – recreational and educational facilities
>> – transport
>> – adaptations to property
>> – holidays
>> – meals, and
>> – telephone facilities.

The Act was taken through Parliament as a private member's bill, which meant that resources could not be made available as part of the legislation. Those who passed the Act argued that it was more important to get the principle accepted.

The procedures by which need was identified, and the level of provision, varied between authorities, and there is little consistency in policy. However, substantial numbers of people are helped. In 1984, there were approximately 371,000 people supplied with personal aids, and over 100,000 telephone rentals paid for by the local authorities. Holidays have been used as a way of providing respite for carers, but the numbers of people helped have fallen from 103,200 in 1976 to 66,400 in 1984. One of the most important aspects of the 1970 Act is that it is the main source of assistance for elderly disabled people, and as such it represents much of what is available for most disabled people.

Housing

The majority of disabled people are in ordinary housing, which will sometimes be adapted to their needs. Housing provision has suffered unduly from the widespread myth that disabled people are likely to be in wheelchairs — an image encouraged by the symbol used on 'disabled' stickers. But there are probably 200,000 wheelchair users in the country, out of 6 million disabled people, and measures which are suitable for some disabled people are not necessarily appropriate for others. A kitchen with a low sink and cupboards is useful for some wheelchair users but may be a nuisance for anyone who has problems bending, a common complaint in specially adapted or 'mobility' housing. The most common cause of disability is probably arthritis, which usually limits mobility in a different way to a wheelchair (DHSS 1971).

Borsay (1986) argues that many problems stem from the treatment of housing as a fixed constant, to which people have to adjust, rather than as a variable commodity which can be altered to meet the needs of the individual. Even among the people for whom mobility housing is supposedly designed, there are likely to be problems because the housing is created according to a general pattern. One survey, for the Department of the Environment, showed that a quarter of the respondents had problems with the doors in mobility housing, and a tenth had problems with corridors (cited in Borsay, pp. 73-77). When aids and adaptations are made to the houses, they tend to conform to fixed, well-established practice rather than meeting individual needs. Blaxter comments that it might be appropriate

> to have showers installed instead of useless baths, or to have coal fires replaced, or to obtain assistance for the alteration of outdated power systems which would not carry labour-saving electrical equipment ... The provision of adaptations was generally confined [in her survey] to certain well-defined, unequivocally "medical" and relatively cheap things, such as rails, ramps and adapted w.c.s. (1976, p. 71).

The main reservation to be made about this, a reservation which Borsay recognises, is that individual adaptations are liable to be expensive.

It can be argued that the emphasis on adaptation is a distraction from the central issues. The problems that disabled people have in common are not so much their physical capacities, which are often very different, but limitations on their life style. Income tends to be low, partly because many disabled people are old and female, partly because they may have special income needs, and because long-term sickness late in someone's working life undermines financial security as they grow older. Socially, disabled people may become isolated, as their health declines, they struggle to manage on the resources they have, they have difficulties in visiting people, and other people find it difficult to come to terms with the disability. The contribution that housing can make is not only the physical adaptations associated with mobility housing; housing is both an essential part of material security, and very often the centre of a person's social life. Housing officers have concentrated perhaps too much on the position of the light switches. For a disabled person, the quality of housing, its location, access to facilities and social environment are at least as important.

Chapter 10
Mental illness and mental handicap

Summary. Mental illness and mental handicap are very different types of condition, with little direct relationship. Mental illnesses lead to differences in thought processes, communication, emotions, and behaviour; the responses may be medical or social, and there are a range of services, mainly concentrated on health, personal social services and housing, which can help mentally ill people. Mental handicap is a problem mainly of slow intellectual development; the emphasis in services tends to be on education and training, and support for carers. Although the two types of condition have so little in common, policies in the past often treated them as if they were equivalent, leading now to common practical problems in the management of the discharge of people from residential care.

Mental illness

'Mental illness' is a broad term covering a range of conditions. The most important are:

Functional psychoses, mainly schizophrenia and manic depression. Schizophrenia is itself a set of conditions rather than a single illness. It is characterised by a complex group of symptoms including, for example, a clouding of consciousness, disconnected speech and thought, variations of mood, feelings that one is being externally controlled, and hallucinations (which can be auditory, visual or tactile).

Schizophrenia comes nearest to the traditional picture of 'madness', though it should not be assumed that schizophrenics are necessarily violent or unpredictable; on the contrary, many are totally disabled, finding it difficult to perform relatively simple tasks. The condition is usually treated with drugs, which when successful have the effect of changing the speed and intensity of thought processes, in order to enable schizophrenic patients to control and order their thoughts. There is also a view that schizophrenia is not a 'disease' or illness, but rather a reaction to intolerable circumstances — a form of flight from reality.

Manic depression leads to severe and sometimes prolonged extremes of mood: in 'manic' phases, constantly active and extrovert, and possibly quite destructive; in depressed state, withdrawn and negative. Drug therapy can be used against the cycle, though again it has been argued that depression is best understood and responded to in social terms. There is considerable evidence to link depression with problems of social isolation and poor environment (Brown & Harris, 1978).

Organic psychoses, caused by infections, drugs, metabolic disturbances, or brain traumas. These can produce symptoms similar to schizophrenia.

Neuroses, including anxiety states, phobias, obsessional states, and some depressions.

'Behavioural' disorders. These are not viewed as 'illness' in the same way. Probably the most important of these is psychopathy, which is characterised mainly by a lack of social awareness, consideration, or conscience towards others.

Mental illness can be seen as primarily a set of medical or physiological conditions; however, because it is identified through the behaviour of the mentally ill person, it can also be seen as social. The importance of this view is that environment may be believed to have an effect on the pattern and severity of a person's mental illness. If schizophrenia is a flight from an unacceptable reality, then one way of dealing with it might be to change the reality (which may be one reason why people who get better while in hospital break down again after they are returned to the community). If depression is a response to isolation and an unsatisfactory environment, the depression might be resolved by a change in the environment — rehousing, which changes not only the person's immediate surroundings, but the pattern of their social relationships.

Services for mentally ill people

Hudson (1982) refers to services for 'psychiatric patients' rather than mentally ill people. The point is an important one; many psychiatric patients are not mentally ill at the time when they are discharged, and many people with mental illnesses never receive psychiatric help.

Treatment. The most common form of treatment for mental illness is based on the use of drugs. The 'drug revolution' of the 1950s made it possible for a number of conditions, particularly schizophrenia and manic depression, to be controlled, even though they cannot be definitively 'cured' in the sense of removing both the symptoms of the illness and its cause. It is difficult to evaluate treatments, because in many cases of mental illness there is a spontaneous remission — that is, the person ceases to behave abnormally anyway.

Although mental illness is treated medically, it is not always certain that the medical model offers the most appropriate response. Psychologists and social workers may contribute to treatment in a number of ways. They include, for example, individual counselling, behavioural therapy, social skills training, family therapy and group therapy. The effectiveness of such measures depends to a large extent on whether the person's mental disorder can be seen as social or behavioural.

Commitment to institutions. Although most mental patients are admitted voluntarily, mentally ill people can be committed to hospital if they are considered a danger to themselves or to others, and appear to be suffering from a mental illness which is susceptible to treatment. In general, committal requires the signature of either the nearest relative or an approved social worker, and one or two doctors. One doctor is required in the case of committal in emergencies, which can be for up to three days (s. 4 of the 1983 Mental Health Act); two doctors are required in other cases, either for assessment (s.2: up to 28 days) or treatment (s. 3: up to six months).

In practice, formal commitment plays only a limited part in the role of mental health services, although the threat of formal commitment may encourage people to accept treatment 'voluntarily' for fear of something worse.

Social reactions to mental illness. Much mental illness is not identified, and consequently not treated. There is considerable resistance to the idea that a person is mentally ill, and often there is resistance to seeking any help. In large part, this is because 'mental illness' is seen as a stigmatising label. Phillips (1963), in researches in the United States, found that people who seek help for mental illness experience a degree of rejection according to the help they seek; a person who consulted a friend was rejected less than someone with the same symptoms who consulted a doctor, the person consulting a doctor less than someone who consulted a psychiatrist. At the same time, a person who had been in a psychiatric institution, but who had no symptoms, was likely to be rejected more than someone who exhibited some quite serious symptoms of mental illness but who had not sought professional help (Phillips 1966). This is not very surprising; the person who has been in an institution is 'labelled', and there may reasonably be some uncertainty as to how that person will behave in the future. But it should not be taken to mean that the label is all-important. Mentally ill people are visible as much through their behaviour as through the medical response to their condition, and Segal, reviewing the literature on attitudes towards mental illness, concludes that 'the behaviour itself, or the pattern of behaviour, is the major determinant of the positive or negative character of the public's attitudes towards mental illness' (1978).

It is often suggested that if people understood mental illness better, they would reject it less. Perhaps surprisingly, this seems not to be true. In a classic study in the United States, Cumming and Cumming (1957) found that members of the public were more negative in their attitudes to mental illness after a programme of community education than before it. The members of the public had a higher initial tolerance of disturbed behaviour than the psychiatrists in the programme did. However, they also made a strong distinction between people who were *ill* and those who were not. The effect of learning about mental illness was to define the limits of acceptable behaviour more clearly and strictly, and so to increase the degree of rejection. There is a clear dilemma here in community education. If mental illness is described as a set of disorders of varying degrees of severity which can affect anyone, it increases the uncertainty and anxiety associated with the concept. On the other hand, if psychiatry is represented as a precise science, it may emphasise the dichotomy between mental illness and 'normal' behaviour. Among the Cummings' respondents, the confidence that mental illness could be treated 'scientifically' made the problem of rejection worse, because they expected patients to be isolated until they were 'cured'.

This says something about the role of mental institutions. Mental institutions were initially designed, not to treat people who were mentally ill — there was no effective treatment — but to isolate them from the community. What is surprising in the developments of recent years is not that some people resist the siting of hostels and group homes near them — a problem sometimes referred to as NIMBY, or 'Not In My Back Yard' — but that the idea has achieved such acceptance.

After care. A care plan is made for each person prior to discharge from hospital. The aim of the plan is to ensure that a discharged patient is able to function normally and independently in the community to the greatest extent possible. The social worker reviews the person's ability to cope, relationships, and material circumstances.

In theory, this should mean that no one is 'dumped' in the community without support, a recurring problem over the last twenty five years. In practice, it is more difficult to provide support in the community than may at first appear from a care plan. Arrangements may break down. People who offer help informally cannot always be relied on to give it. A family which offers support in the belief that the patient has been 'cured' may recoil when they find a difficult situation. The discharged patients may not always co-operate with the care plan, and often fail to keep appointments or fail to tell the authorities about changes in their situation. It has not been uncommon for former mental patients to become vagrants, lacking not only a home but also the finance, medical care and social contacts for which a home provides the basis. The evidence of the Church Army to the House of Commons Social Services Committee was that over a quarter of the thousand people in their hostels had been discharged from mental hospitals.

It is also important to recognise that many people who are being discharged into the community are acutely ill. This case, sadly all too typical, is from an article in *The Guardian:*

> 'Robert is a 25-year-old schizophrenic. He lives alone but cannot look after himself. Just over a month ago he turned up at Hackney Hospital's psychiatric outpatients clinic nearly starving. He had not eaten for two days. Robert simply cannot cope with everyday details of life in the community. He suffers from hallucinations which terrify him and which progressively damage his mind. He cannot think straight, let alone manage to budget ...' (Pope, 1988).

The role of housing services
A range of options have been developed for housing psychiatric patients.

The services are very diverse, which is very important, in view of the wide range of needs. The options include:

— hostels equipped to deal with psychiatric care, including medical support and drug therapy.

— staffed hostels, or 'half-way houses'. They are, perhaps surprisingly, not widely available for people with mental illnesses, a limitation which reflects resources rather than needs. Although they are intended to be a stage between hospital and ordinary housing, in practice it may be difficult to move people on, and residents stay there for long periods by default.

— 'group homes', or shared housing. Group homes are organised without a resident member of staff; Gibbons notes that although staff may visit weekly, they were likely to take on a role 'more like that of an ordinary landlord than any other' (1988, p.184). Initially, group homes were intended to act as a transitional stage for residents. In practice it can be difficult to settle a new person in with existing residents, and the homes have become permanent (Ritchie & Keegan, 1983).

— cluster homes. The principle here is that a number of people live in reasonably close proximity, but not necessarily in an identifiable unit, and receive support from workers who travel out to them. 'Core and cluster homes', as the name suggests, consist of a core unit which also serves other units further away.

— boarding out, or substitute family care. This is not extensively used for psychiatric patients.

— ordinary housing.

Research for the DoE emphasises the importance of flexibility, professional support, the availability of appropriate counselling for residents, and very careful selection (Ritchie & Keegan, 1983).

In providing for people who have had psychiatric problems, housing officers need to bear certain principles in mind. Firstly, people who are recovering from mental illness have to be seen as specially vulnerable. There is a risk of relapse. This is particularly true if the mental illness is social in origin, a reaction to stress or isolation. Second, the development of a treatment plan and maintenance of support within the community often depend crucially on the availability and location of accommodation. This may reflect social needs, but it may also be true because people are unable to receive appropriate medical support within their present accommodation — and a patient who does not receive medication is liable to suffer, not simply a psychiatric breakdown, but at the same time a breakdown of social relationships. Many psychiatric patients become homeless. Third, housing may itself be a cause of mental illness. If mental illness can result in some cases from environmental factors, then housing, as one of the most important elements in a person's environment, can make a major contribution to a person's mental state.

Mental handicap

'Mental handicap' refers to a state of retarded intellectual development.

A person who is mentally handicapped is slow to develop. Although it is sometimes associated with other conditions — a high proportion of severely mentally handicapped people are also severely physically handicapped — most has no physical or organic origin. (Down's syndrome, probably the best known cause, accounts for only about one sixth of all cases.) The problem of mental handicap is often treated as a medical one, and the assessment of mental handicap falls within the remit of medical services, as does mental handicap nursing and care. But it is not an illness, and it is not susceptible to medical 'treatment' or cure.

Mental handicap is sometimes referred to in terms of a person's 'IQ', or 'Intelligence Quotient'. Average intelligence is measured as an IQ of 100; a person with an IQ of less than 70 would be considered mentally handicapped, and a person with an IQ of less than 50 would be considered severely mentally handicapped. This sort of measurement is of limited usefulness, because there is little clear relationship between the numbers being used and what they mean in practice. When the idea of IQ was developed, it was supposed to be a measure of a person's 'mental age', a term which seems to imply a set capacity. Although a person can become mentally handicapped as an adult, usually through an accident causing brain damage, much of mental handicap stems from a very early age, and the problems of slow development build over time. A person of eight who is severely mentally handicapped cannot meaningfully be compared with an average child aged one, two, four or six; the nature of the handicap changes the pattern of behaviour altogether. In the first place, normal children are curious, responsive, and quick to learn; a child who does not behave in the same way is different in that alone. Secondly, mentally handicapped children have different physical abilities from children who are mentally at a similar stage of development. Many mentally handicapped children are labelled 'hyperactive' because they have not learned social restraints but have a destructive potential far in advance of a very young child. Thirdly, as the child grows physically, the nature of the tasks that the child has to learn are different. Most children learn to walk at a particular stage of their development; by the time some mentally handicapped children are ready to learn to walk, their muscular and physical structure is not the same as those of a child of one or two years.

These problems of development constitute a major challenge to the family — or, to be more precise, the women in the family, because it is to women that the responsibility for child care generally falls. The family has to cope with a child which is dependent for a long period, not only because of limited mental capacity, but because this limited mental capacity leads in turn to associated problems of physical capacity and social behaviour. Children take much longer to learn to walk, to feed themselves, to bath themselves, to use a toilet; at the same time, they are becoming stronger and heavier. Much of the support which a carer needs is with the physical burden this creates — what Bayley (1973) calls the 'daily grind'. But it is often the case that little help is forthcoming; services are stretched and wholly inadequate to the purpose. In part, this is because insufficient attention has been paid to the problems of carers. But it is also true that the

the level of care required is so great, and takes up so much of the day, that it is difficult to see how the state could practically meet it within a normal domestic environment, rather than in residential institutions.

Services for mentally handicapped people

From 0–5, the main statutory responsibility falls on Social Services, although in practice the health service is liable to play a major role, because of the need to assess the problem. In many cases, the primary contact in early stages is a health visitor. It is possible, if unusual, to enter education from the age of 2. The voluntary sector also plays a major role, reflecting the inadequacy of the statutory services.

The aim of social work with mentally handicapped people has been seen primarily as a remit to support the work of families. The services provided include counselling parents and relatives, providing information, aids and appliances to help with specific problems, respite care — that is, short term residential provision or fostering, and organising recreation, breaks or holidays. Much of the work is considered to be at a low level and it tends to be delegated to social work assistants.

From 5 to 18 the education service is principally liable for the mentally handicapped person. The move to education is relatively recent — it stems from a major policy change in 1970, intended to emphasise the view that mentally handicapped people are educable and do need special resources to help with their development. In practice 5 to 16 is much more common, with many education authorities failing to provide facilities to mentally handicapped people over 16. Schooling may take place in ordinary schools, special schools, or hospitals.

The situation for a mentally handicapped adult is often very different from that of a child. It would be a mistake to compare them in this with children; they are adults, and have many of the social influences and emotional pressures that adults do. Although some will still be limited in their physical abilities, by the time they have become adults many mentally handicapped people have learned a number of basic skills. They may still have difficulties, for example, with literacy, handling money, or social behaviour. From 18 (or 16) onwards, the responsibility for mentally handicapped adults returns to Social Services. Social Services provide Adult Training Centres (or 'Social Education Centres'). (Malin et al (1980) are highly critical of most ATCs, which they see as lacking adequate facilities or training, and having no clear objectives for individual clients. There has been some movement — the policy of Warwickshire is exemplary — but in many areas it is limited.)

This system of support has the unfortunate effect of passing statutory responsibility back and forth between services. To improve co-ordination, the Warnock report, which was concerned with educational needs, suggested that each child should have a 'named person' who would be the primary contact for a family over a long period. Although the principle was accepted in the 1981 Education Act, it does not seem to have been implemented in any meaningful way.

The role of housing services

The role of housing services in response to mentally handicapped people may at first sight seem limited. Housing is not a cause of mental handicap, and cannot been seen directly as part of the response to it; it may seem inappropriate, then, to refer to 'mental handicap' as a special need for housing. But this would be to take too narrow a view. Housing constitutes, firstly, a vital part of the support network for families, on whom care for mentally handicapped people principally depends. Second, mentally handicapped people are made specially vulnerable by their circumstances, and are liable in a competitive market to find themselves in inferior housing on unfavourable terms. Housing services have still, for mentally handicapped people, a protective role, a role which was once a central feature of social housing, but which over time has become less important in relation to other groups.

The range of options for housing mentally handicapped people is similar to the range for mentally ill people. It includes:

- hostels equipped to deal with special medical or nursing needs. This is most appropriate when a mentally handicapped person has physical needs in addition to mental handicap, either because of physical disability, or because the mental handicap has prevented that person from learning basic self-care, like dressing, feeding or toileting. In a supportive, educative environment, these skills can be learned, though it is a labour-intensive activity to teach them.
- staffed hostels. They are widely used for people with mental handicaps. They may be appropriate to a wide range of needs, from those who may have learned basic self-care but who have not necessarily learned the skills for independent living, like cooking or handling money, to others who have learned these skills in large part but require a degree of social support.
- colonies. The principle of the 'village' for mentally handicapped people, organised by some voluntary organisations, is not as popular as it was, because it is seen as isolating people from the community; but it represents an option favoured by some people.
- 'group homes', or shared housing. The size of group homes has gradually reduced over the years; there used to be group homes with about 12 people, but four is now the usual maximum (Atkinson 1988). This option is clearly most favoured for the most independent mentally handicapped people, who have a sufficient range of skills of self-management but who may require monitoring and some support available on hand in the event of difficulties.
- cluster homes. The great advantage of cluster homes is that they deploy staffing to help people with a range of needs, with those who are least independent in the core home, and those best able to manage able to draw on the support of the specialist staff.
- boarding out. This can range to a form of substitute family care, to a supportive lodging scheme; the programme will depend on the needs of the individual.
- ordinary housing.

The appropriate scheme depends greatly on the circumstances and preferences of the people affected.

There are potential problems in setting up facilities for mentally handicapped people, because the 'Not In My Back Yard' syndrome applies here almost as much as it does in the case of mental illness. This reaction to a housing association scheme is from the Nottingham Evening Post:

> 'Families in a Nottingham suburb are trying to block plans to move five mentally handicapped people into a £70,000 bungalow. More than 70 people ... have put up thousands of pounds for a barrister to fight the move through the courts. The residents' action group say it is the lack of consultation they object to. ... Mr Martin Pickering, who is general manager of Highbury Hospital, said: "We would refute the view that there have not been any consultations. The residents are making matters difficult by insisting talks take place through a solicitor." '
> (Tyrell 1988)

Policies for mentally ill and mentally handicapped people

It may seem strange that mental illness and mental handicap are considered within the same chapter — and if it does not, it should have done. The conditions are so different, and the responses to them have so little in common, that there seems to be no obvious connection. However, though the two terms refer to very different types of condition, it has often been true that policy for mental disorder has been founded on an irrational, and to some extent an illegitimate, association between them.

'Degeneracy', a term related primarily to mental handicap, was believed, at the turn of the century, to be at the root of many of the problems of society. Idiocy, insanity, crime and pauperism were all attributable to people who were flawed from birth. The Eugenics Society, which put forward such ideas strongly, was to have a major influence on the 1913 Mental Deficiency Act, which classified mentally handicapped people not only as idiots, imbeciles, morons or feeble-minded, but also as 'morally defective', a term which was used, for example, to cover young girls who had illegitimate children. The Act remained in force until 1959; some of the people admitted under it are still in institutions, others are in the process of being discharged.

Many mental institutions were originally built with the intention of isolating 'degenerates' from the community. The buildings were often deliberately built in outlying locations, effectively cut off from the outside world. They were used to contain both mental illness and mental handicap. Effectively, this means that the two groups have not only a shared history, but also a set of common problems — the problems which come from living in institutions, and the process of discharge.

Institutional care

Wolfensberger (1972) argues, in respect of mental handicap, that many of the problems of mental institutions stem from a view of residents as animals, a view which runs through much of the provision.

1. The assumption of primitive and uncontrolled behaviour leads to the creation of 'abuse-resistant' areas.
2. Residents are assumed to be destructive and ready to assault others. The emphasis is on custody and order.
3. They are assumed to be incapable of choice. Lights and temperature are controlled and out of reach.
4. Animals have to be kept. Wards are organised for supervision, not for people to live on.
5. They are assumed to be dirty. There are often mass cleaning facilities.
6. Animals are ineducable, so no opportunities are necessary for development.
7. Animals have no aesthetic sense. Wards are often dull and poorly decorated.
8. There is no need for privacy, property, communication with others or individuality. Animals have no rights.

This may seem exaggerated, but the view it represents is supported by a long line of scandals in mental institutions, used both for mentally ill and mentally handicapped people. The first of these was in Ely Hospital in Cardiff in 1967, where there were accusations of cruelty, inhumane treatment, and pilfering by staff. This was not substantiated, but there were 'old-fashioned, unduly rough and undesirably low standards of nursing care'. Ely had isolated buildings, overcrowded wards, a shortage of staff, and patients confined for much of the time (see Cmnd 3795, 1969). Pauline Morris, in *Put Away* (1969), showed that many of these problems were general in institutions. The Government's response to the 1969 report on Ely included a policy document, *Better Services for the mentally handicapped* (Cmnd 4683), published in 1971. Nevertheless, scandals continued. In 1971, cruelty at Farleigh hospital led to prison sentences. A report on Whittingham hospital in 1972 identified neglect, petty corruption, restraint of patients, cruelty and a failure of supervision. In 1974, a report on South Ockenden hospital also referred to violence, cruelty and the seclusion of patients, to a background of overcrowded wards, lack of facilities, inadequate numbers of staff, nurses unable to speak English, queues of naked patients for baths and w.c.'s open to corridors. *Opening the door,* by Kathleen Jones (1975), surveyed a number of hospitals and found for example that two-thirds of wards had no curtains dividing the residents' beds, and that in most wards less than half the residents had any possessions. In 1978, the Normansfield report (Cmnd 7357), probably the most thorough and horrifying of these investigations, showed, while mainly concentrating on the malpractice of a consultant psychiatrist and a strike by nursing staff, poor buildings, patients having to be moved because of leaking roofs, 'appalling' standards of hygiene, lack of privacy, bare wards, 'degrading' dress, lack of possessions, a total lack of stimulation, heavy sedation of patients and the dominance of control over care. The list of scandals and exposés goes on: it includes, e.g., Rampton, Brookwood, St Lawrence's, St Matthew's. Martin's book *Hospitals in Trouble* (1984) provides a detailed, disturbing account.

The development of services for mental illness led, in the 1950s and 1960s, to an increasing emphasis on treating people in the community. This was encouraged, in the first place, by disillusion with the role played by large institutions, marked by the Royal Commission on the Law relating to Mental Illness and Deficiency (Cmnd 169, 1957), whose report led to the 1959 Mental Health Act. Barton, in *Institutional Neurosis* (1959) described a condition brought on by the regime of institutions. Goffman, in *Asylums* (1959, published in Britain in 1961) explained apparently disturbed behaviour, like hoarding rubbish, in terms of a reaction to a 'total' environment. Secondly, a 'drug revolution' had made it possible to control the behaviour of mentally ill people in the community. This was used (irrationally) to justify arguments for the discharge of both mentally ill and mentally handicapped people. Third, there had been a substantial increase in the cost of institutional care. Scull, in *Decarceration* (1984), argues that this is the crucial element; arguments against institutions had been made in the previous century without effect, because at that time supervision in institutions was cheaper.

Enoch Powell, as Minister of Health in 1961, looked forward to the closure of all mental institutions. A Hospital Plan in 1962 was followed in 1963 by the first plans for community care. This was only the beginning of a process, seeking to discharge people from institutions, which has recently been accelerated (see Jones 1972).

The use of institutional care has accordingly changed. Psychiatric patients are now more likely to be dealt with in psychiatric wards in general hospitals. Mentally handicapped people, however, may still require long-term care. The emphasis on funding for services for mentally handicapped people after 1976 in large part reflects concern with these problems. *Better Services* recognised the issues and argued for a more 'homelike' environment offering 'sympathetic and consistent human relationships'. The National Development Group for the Mentally Handicapped argued for new standards of care, including e.g. maximum units of 12 adults or 6 children and staff ratios of 1 to 3 (see, e.g., NDGMH, 1980). The Jay Report on Mental Handicap Nursing and Care (Cmnd 7468, 1979) argued for the creation of a new profession of mental handicap nursing; this was strongly opposed by the Royal College of Nursing, which saw it as a reflection on their profession, and most of the proposals were decently buried. Since then, mental handicap nursing has been developing as a specialism within the nursing profession.

Community care

Much of the move towards community care has to be seen as a reaction to the problems of institutions. The imprecision of the concept makes it difficult to evaluate. Reference is frequently made to 'support' in the community, but it is not always clear what support is needed, or who should provide it.

This imprecision reflects, too, the wide range of needs that are referred to under the umbrella of 'community care'. Mentally ill people do not have one need, or one set of needs, in common; different responses are appropriate for different types of problem. Equally, mentally handicapped people cannot be treated as a uniform group all with similar needs; there is an enormous difference between the needs of a family with a severely mentally handicapped child at the age of 5, and a single mentally handicapped adult at the age of 18. If there is no common set of needs, it is equally clear that there can be no common response.

In many ways, the Griffiths report (1988) reflects this confusion when it argues that support should be mainly provided by one agency — the social services department. It is one thing to suggest that a particular agency should have the principal responsibility for co-ordinating the efforts of different services, and in assuring that services are delivered to the individual from various sources. It is another entirely to suggest that any one agency is capable, within the present structure, of delivering the services itself; and this is the trap Griffiths falls into, by suggesting that Social Services Departments should take responsibility for many more aspects of services dealing with community care.

There may still be a case for a single, specialised service to deal with aspects of community care for mentally ill or handicapped people. The advantages of such an arrangement are, first, that it would be possible to plan nationally for priorities and expenditure for the groups, and second, that specialised arrangements create the opportunity to develop expertise and appropriate models of provision. The main disadvantages are that no service is equipped to deal with every need, and other services cannot be relieved of their responsibilities towards the client group. Community care consists, necessarily, of a range of services delivered in a variety of contexts. If the arguments at the beginning of Part 3 are right, the most appropriate form of response is one which is co-ordinated between members of a multi-disciplinary team.

Chapter 11
Children in need

Summary. The response to children in need has moved away from a structural response to a pathological model requiring intervention at the level of the family. In the process, housing has been marginalised as an influence; but housing clearly still has a major impact on the welfare of families, and a large role to play. This may also be true at the individual level; the Tyra Henry case indicates that housing agencies may be considered responsible, as social workers have been, for failing to respond in cases of child abuse.

Family policy

The treatment of children has to be understood in the context of the role of the family. Children are considered to be the responsibility of families, and the constitution of the family is governed by a powerful set of social rules and expectations. If children are deprived or neglected, it is on the face of the matter the responsibility of the family, not of the state; the state services are designed to complement the role of the family, not to replace it.

Even though there are strong values protecting the family, there are other equally strong social pressures for state intervention on behalf of children. The deprivation suffered by children was one of the first areas to attract state intervention, with the introduction of school meals in 1906. Intervention in the family, through the development of visits to mothers and babies, became common in the period after the First World War.

The reasons why this should be true are not difficult to establish. In the first place, children are considered particularly vulnerable; it is in respect of children that the model of institutional welfare, arguing that everyone is likely to be dependent, is most powerful. Secondly, the very strength of the moral norms protecting children and the family gives the issues a high degree of prominence whenever they come to public notice; examples are the many scandals following serious cases of child abuse, like Maria Colwell, Jasmine Beckford, or the Cleveland inquiry into the sexual abuse of children. Thirdly, there is a clear social interest in providing for children. The introduction of school meals was justified in part on the basis of 'national efficiency'; one third of the recruits for the Boer War had been turned away because they were unhealthy, and the main cause of ill health was malnutrition. When family allowances were introduced after the Second World War (by a coalition government dominated by the Conservatives) one of the arguments for doing so was to try to prevent the reduction in the population that was feared, because of the implications this would have for the nation as a whole. (Other nations, in the same period, went much further. France's allowances for children, and in particular for 'familles nombreuses', are far more generous than Britain's. In the Soviet Union, Stalin introduced 'mother hero' medals for particularly prolific producers.)

Despite the emphasis on child care, however, there is no clear policy for children in Britain. In part, this is because child care is held to be the responsibility of the family; but, perhaps surprisingly, there is no clear policy for the family either. What there is, rather, is a set of policies which may affect families, which is a very different matter. In some cases, the policies which are followed reflect social norms about the family. The assumptions about the family and child support are most strongly challenged by feminists, who argue that the effect of many of these policies is to force women into a particular mode, and to penalise those who do not fit it. The education system has been accused of imposing a stereotyped role on women, both formally by pushing girls into following certain types of study, and informally, through social contact and expectations about what girls are like and what they should do (see Finch 1984). In social security, there is an assumption that women are likely to be dependent on their husbands. Beveridge treated married women who were working as a special category, which was already questionable at the time he was writing; he made provision for widows, because they had lost the breadwinner; he recognised that some people might be divorced, but thought that it was not an insurable risk. One of the most important rules in social security assuming dependency on a breadwinner is the 'cohabitation rule'. Since married women depend on their husbands, they are not able to claim most benefits in their own right. The cohabitation rule is intended to make sure that couples who are not married are not treated more favourably than couples who are. A couple who are 'living together as man and wife' are assumed to share financial resources. This has some curious moral implications. Phillips (1981), writing about the system in the US, points out that, from the point of view of economics, a cohabitation rule penalises people with a stable relationship, but not those who are promiscuous; it discourages mothers from entering a relationship which will lead to marriage; it encourages mothers to separate from fathers, and discourages fathers from child support.

The 'cycle of deprivation'

The problems of children in need were for many years interpreted exclusively as the problems of children in poverty. At the time of the foundation of the welfare state, the main cause of deprivation was interpreted as being material: a new emphasis on education, income and housing would deal with many of the problems.

The apparent failure of the welfare state to deal with the central problems led to increased attention on the families which were producing deprived children. *Born to fail,* by Wedge and Prosser (1973), shows the accumulated disadvantages of some children relative to others. It is based on the National Child Development Survey, which followed through the progress of over 10,000 children. At the age of eleven, the most disadvantaged children were those living in either large or single parent families with low income and bad housing. The vast majority were working class. The children lacked basic amenities in the home, and were likely to share beds. They were shorter than other children, more likely to be absent from school because of ill health, more subject to accidents of any kind, more likely to suffer impairment of vision, hearing or speech, to be treated as 'maladjusted', to be of low educational ability and to be in special education. They were over ten times as likely as others to be in the care of the local authority.

Keith Joseph, as Secretary of State for Social Services, put forward the idea of a 'cycle of deprivation', in which poor parents were likely to have children who would in turn be poor. Inadequate parenting led to multiple disadvantages, or 'transmitted deprivation'; the children would become inadequate parents in turn. In many ways, Joseph's view seems to be common sense; but common sense is wrong. Joseph also, to his credit, set up a working party to research into the issue. Ten years later, it reported that there was no good evidence to show that this actually happened. On the contrary, most poor children are not themselves poor as adults; and although it is widely believed that there are some families in which multiple deprivations continue from generation to generation, there was surprisingly little evidence to bear this out (Brown & Madge, 1982).

The idea of the 'cycle of deprivation' can be seen as the direct descendant of the idea of the 'problem family'. The emphasis in the literature on the 'problem family' usually falls on the family's way of life, the neglect of children, and defective mental capacity (Philp & Timms, 1957). The concept of the 'problem family' has its origins in the idea of 'degeneracy' — one of the principal pieces of written work (Blacker 1952) was produced by the Eugenics Society. According to Blacker, problem families exhibit five 'commonly recognised' features. First is mental subnormality, which presumes a link between social problems and mental handicap. Under the 1913 Mental Deficiency Act, 'moral defectives' — who might include promiscuous girls, or unmarried mothers — were put in institutions. Some of them are still there, or in the process of discharge. Secondly, there is temperamental instability, which implies that these families are liable to be unpredictable, or even violent. Third, they are ineducable; the problem family cannot be improved. Fourth, they have a squalid home; the family is dirty. Lastly, there is the presence of numerous children. Problem families breed prolifically and are unable to restrain themselves.

There are some families which do have an high number of problems, but hardly any have all of these features, and the evidence is that families like this are extremely rare (Rutter & Madge 1976; Brown & Madge 1982), so rare as to suggest the idea is more concerned with myth than with fact. The myth is an important one, because it affects the way that people behave towards supposed 'problem families'. Problem families were defined, not only by their nuisance value, but also by the assumption that the family was degenerate, and therefore incapable of change or improvement, and unable to respond if they were treated well. Macey and Baker write:

> No reorganisation of administration, no application of technical skill, can guarantee good results in the community's efforts to convert the small group who form the hard core of problem families into tolerably decent citizens (1982, p.433).

There is no reason whatever to suppose that this is true. The description of the 'problem family' is a catalogue of the prejudices and stigmas of a previous era; the concept has no place in the provision of social services now.

Child care policy

There are, to be sure, some families which do not provide an adequate environment for a child to grow up in, and families in which children may be neglected, exploited or abused. The powers of the state have been largely limited to 'intervention', a term which conceals the assumption that the family is the normal environment for a child, that when a family does not function properly the main function of the state is to maintain the family, and that it is only in extreme and unusual cases that it is necessary to take over those functions. In these cases, the child will be 'taken into care', a term which means that the local authority formally takes over the role of parent. The primary grounds are defined in the Children Act 1980:

- neglect or ill-treatment
- similar treatment of another child in the household, or the presence of an adult who has abused children before
- 'moral danger' to the child
- the child is beyond control
- the child is not receiving an education, or
- the child is guilty of an offence.

The development of services for children has been dominated by a particular model which identified the problems of children who were deprived or abused with the issues concerning young offenders. In part, this reflects a school of thought represented by John Bowlby, whose book *Maternal Care and Mental Health* (1951) emphasised not only the importance of the mother in child development but also its links with deviant behaviour. Bowlby was not, however, the original source of this view; the 1933 Children and Young Persons Act, which made it an offence to assault, ill-treat or neglect a child, also emphasised links between services for neglected and delinquent children, and established 'Approved Schools'.

The link also reflects the influence of the Home Office, which until 1970 was responsible both for child care and for the legal system. The Ingleby Committee (Cmnd. 1191, 1960), which was to recommend the extension of the powers of Childrens Departments to undertake preventive work, was principally concerned with young offenders. The Labour Party's concern with social services was represented, before the 1964 election, by a report entitled *Crime — a challenge to us all,* and the Seebohm committee was set up after a government white paper called *The Child, the Family and the Young Offender* (Cmnd 2742, 1965).

The ultimate reform of the child care system was strongly based in this view. The Children and Young Persons Act 1969 sought to remove any distinction between young offenders and children who had been abused or neglected. Approved schools were replaced by a new system of community homes. The main forms of child care now are:

- placements with the child's own parents or relatives, under supervision (this is used in many cases, including over a third of young offenders in care: Parker, 1988)
- fostering: the use of a temporary substitute family
- adoption: a permanent substitute family
- community homes: residential care for children, and
- community homes with education, which include schooling as well as residential care.

A child who is admitted to care may in many areas be placed initially in an Observation and Assessment Centre, which is intended to assess the most appropriate placement. Fostering and adoption are rarely seen as options for young offenders with a deprived background — they account for only 5% of placements (Parker 1988) — which means that a higher proportion of young offenders are likely to go to residential care; but it is equally true, because of the difficulty of finding foster placements for older children, that children who are neglected or abused are also likely to be placed in a community home. The purpose of the 1969 reforms was an attempt to remove the stigma of criminality from young offenders. The effect has arguably been to transfer the stigma of criminality to everyone else.

Child abuse and neglect

The neglect of a child first became an offence in 1868. The Poor Law Amendment Act made it illegal to fail to provide food, clothing, housing or medical aid for one's child. The concern at that time was to make sure that children should not become a burden on the rates, and it was only in 1933 that ill treatment and neglect were defined as criminal offences.

The Curtis report (Cmd 6922, 1946) was in part a response to a child care scandal — the O'Neill case, where a boy was killed by his foster parents — and in part representative of the move to expand state provision after the War. By the 1948 Children Act, it became the duty of a local authority to 'receive the child into care' when children are orphaned, deserted, their parent or guardian is incapacitated, or the parent was deemed 'unfit' to keep the child. The presumption was (and still is) that voluntary care would be preferred to compulsory admission. There was no power to keep the child in care and a Home Office Circular (HO 160) instructed Childrens Departments to try to keep families together.

The responsibilities of Children's Departments were increased in 1952. By the Children and Young Persons (Amendment) Act, the local authority was given a duty to *investigate* cases of neglect. The Ingleby committee (which sat 1956–1960) recommended that local authorities should become involved in preventive work. This was incorporated in the 1963 Children and Young Persons Act, which included a duty to try to *prevent* abuse or neglect, made it possible to use financial payments (s.1) to avoid children coming into care, and established further grounds on which a child could be taken into care.

The 1969 Children and Young Persons Act redefined the grounds on which a care order could be made. The reorganisation of child care was closely followed by two major reorganisations of social services agencies — the first after 1970, with the creation of new departments, and the second with the reform of local government.

The Colwell case. Maria Colwell was a child who was abused and neglected by her stepfather after she had been returned to her mother from foster care (DHSS 1974). Although the inquiry has been seen as a criticism of social work practice, the report was more important as evidence of major deficiencies in the procedures for dealing with child abuse. A large number of workers had known something about the case — social worker, NSPCC officer, health visitor, GP, police, housing officer — but the information had never been collated.

The main legislative response to the Colwell case was the 1975 Children Act, which was limited in scope and mainly concerned with arrangements for fostering and adoption. The main innovation, custodianship, was not implemented for several years after the Act. The changes to practice were more important. Since Colwell, the norm has been to appoint a 'key worker' to whom all information will be referred. The key worker is usually, though not always, a social worker. The functions of the key worker can be divided between *primary contact* and *role co-ordinator.* The primary contact is the worker most often seen by the family — perhaps a health visitor, probation officer or NSPCC office — and role co-ordination may still be kept within Social Services, so that other workers (police, GP, housing, teachers) will refer to the right place.

The Colwell case also exposed social work to substantial criticism by the press. Child abuse is good copy — sensational, human interest, easy to relate to; it sells newspapers. Subsequent cases of child abuse have been met with extreme criticisms of social work in practice. The following comes from a Daily Mail editorial on the case of Malcolm Page (1980).

Arrogant complacency and a baby's death

Last February, in a filthy upstairs room of a Tilbury house, a baby boy of 13 months was found freezing to death. He had not been fed for six days. His wizened features were those of an old man. The room stank. His urine-encrusted romper suit had to be cut from his body, the temperature of which was 20 degrees below normal. He had lain uncovered in that icy room for at least 12 hours. His legs were purple with ulcers. He had severe gangrene in five toes. Downstairs, while their youngest child was dying this most horrible of deaths, his parents ... were warming themselves by the fire. They are both now warming themselves in Her Majesty's prisons. That is where they deserve to be....

But there are others who carry a heavy burden of responsibility for failing to avert the harrowing tragedy. The Essex Social Services Department were supposed to be keeping a caring eye on the children of this wretchedly inadequate couple. One social worker ... visited the family on no less than 48 occasions in the months before neglect froze the life out of little Malcolm Page. Yet, incredibly, this trained and supposedly experienced young woman saw nothing, heard nothing, smelt nothing to convince her that the baby should be taken away from its parents.

How often was she able to get a good look at the baby? How hard did she try? Why was she never suspicious? Why did she not talk to the neighbours ... ? Why did she not question the home help? We do not know. What we do know is that the attitude [she] now conveys — an attitude backed by her superiors — is one of imperturbability verging on complacency. 'I have no reason to feel guilty', she says ...

The Essex Social Services Department, running true to form, has closed ranks and put up a wall of official spokesmen to announce that no action will be taken. Nobody is to blame. It is no one's fault. Sadly, the Daily Mail predicts that when the next tragic case of a child's terrible death while under the case care of a social worker is revealed, the same arrogant complacency will come into play from the social services department concerned. ...

After the Jasmine Beckford case in 1985, the social workers principally were held to account by the authority (and the director resigned, with the comment that the pressure from the press had been such that she had had to remind herself, when she went to bed at night, that it wasn't her who had killed the child). Some social workers took industrial action in support. The headline in the *Today* newspaper was: 'Social workers dance on little Jasmine's grave.' Needless to say, this sort of coverage has done little for the public image of social work, and it has arguably played a large part in disillusion with the social worker's role.

Perhaps surprisingly, the continuing scandals in child care have had little visible impact on *policy,* as opposed to social work practice. The succession of scandals has led both to a higher number of children coming into care, and a greater concern with paperwork. In the early 1980s, pressure for 'parental rights' increased. The 1983 Health and Social Services etc. Act (HASSASSA) included a statutory code of practice on access to children in care. It has led to an increasing use of Guardian ad Litem social workers, who advise courts on children's interests in contested cases.

Housing and the needs of children

The importance of social housing in this process may not, at first, be clear. When the focus of policy fell on the needs of children, there was no question but that housing was a major element in the life style of families. The main problem was poverty. A child living in unsatisfactory housing conditions clearly suffered important disadvantages in social terms. The child's health was put at risk through conditions which bred disease, such as tuberculosis. The child's education depended on the provision of adequate play space in and around the house, and on somewhere to do homework.

The emphasis on poverty has reduced. The concern with child abuse and neglect has led to a different approach; there is a widespread myth that child abuse is not linked with poverty or poor conditions, but that it can arise equally throughout social classes (the evidence against this belief, mainly from the United States, is given by Parton 1985). The myth has been used, Parton argues, to reinforce an individualistic, psychologically oriented view of these problems. In the process, the importance of material factors like housing seems to have been reduced. But this is not necessarily the way that it appears to the social workers involved with the families. Social work with children and families is primarily concerned with risk. The social workers' task is not primarily to monitor a child's condition; they do not have the power to do so. Social workers have no rights of entry to a person's home; they are not medically trained; they do not have the power to examine children physically (though the inquiry into the case of Jasmine Beckford [Blom-Cooper et al 1985] seemed to imply that they should). What they have to do is something far less tangible, and much more difficult to assess. They are supposed to identify the degree of risk which a child has, and to take steps to reduce that risk.

There are several ways in which a social worker might believe that housing is a major part of the this process. In the first place, bad housing may itself cause problems. Depression can lead someone to neglect a child. Frustration, it is often believed, leads to aggression. People living in overcrowded, insecure accommodation may react to stress by violence.

Secondly, housing is a major part of a family's social life. The support people have depends very much on their social contact, and social contact in turn depends on where they live and what sort of place they live in. If a family lives near enough to parents or friends who can help with child care, for example, many of the problems which stem from inadequate parenting can be alleviated.

Thirdly, a lack of adequate housing can obstruct any attempts to deal with other problems. The client's understanding of what the social worker is doing is often very different from the social worker's. Clients come to social workers for help. It may be surprising to people outside Social Services Departments, but that help is not necessarily forthcoming. Social Services Departments have a wide remit, but there are limits to it, and social workers do not do everything. They are certainly not all-purpose advocates who pick up the 'phone on behalf of every person who walks through the door. But there are cases in which the social worker might well consider it is appropriate to begin by seeking to establish a person's financial or housing status. The social worker is expected to assess the case, and assessment is impossible if the case is cluttered with the debris of a huge range of problems. How can one reasonably assess a person's ability to cope with a child if everyone is living in one room and they don't have enough food to eat?

Housing officers often do not respond to requests of social workers for help with families at risk. In part, this reflects a misunderstanding of the social worker's role; social workers are seen in the same light as any other person putting a case on behalf of the individual. In part, it happens because the problems which social workers are dealing with are not the sort of problems which are recognised as constituting 'housing need'. Housing need is viewed as somehow objective and measurable. Risk, in its very nature, is intangible, and often unprovable — until the worst happens.

The Tyra Henry case
In one case of child abuse, the case of Tyra Henry, criticisms that were made of the failure of social workers were extended directly to the housing department. The details are worth considering; the implications for housing management, if the argument of the report is accepted, cannot be underestimated.

Tyra Henry was in the care of the London Borough of Lambeth because of the violence of her father, who eventually killed her. Tyra and her mother, Claudette, relied mainly on Beatrice, Claudette's mother, for support, and Beatrice had virtually taken over Tyra's care. Beatrice's accommodation was damp and overcrowded, making it difficult for Claudette to stay there. The social worker argued for rehousing, emphasising the element of risk to the child. The intention was to place Tyra with Beatrice, where she would be safe, and to move Claudette near to them, where she would be able to maintain contact with Tyra and in time take over again as Tyra's mother.

The housing department did not act at once. Beatrice was in arrears of rent, and her application to move in November 1982 was blocked for nearly a year. In June 1983, the social worker made representations to the department about the risk from the father. The department, in their evidence to the inquiry, said that these representations were

> Noted, but as never raised by tenant as connected with transfer nor confirmatory information received nor further contact by DSS (social services) or household until February 1984, no further action was taken (Sedley et al, 1987, p.42).

This seems to imply that they would only have taken it seriously if the social worker, the client and the Social Services hierarchy had badgered them over a period of time. The social worker clearly felt it was pointless to try to do so, and the inquiry is scathing about the housing department's attitude:

> There is a constant sense of near-impotence in relation to housing: rather than being an essential and reliable adjunct of social work, it appears from social services' standpoint like the weather, always there, often unpredictable and entirely beyond influence or control. We can understand how this came about ... but we also consider that a less fatalistic approach to housing in the present

case would have yielded significant results.... Nevertheless, the reaction of the housing departments ... was obtuse enough ... to give ample grounds for the gloom which surrounded social services' dealings with them (ibid, pp. 44-45).

Ultimately, the plan which the social worker had made for Tyra's care collapsed, in large part because adequate housing was not available; and Tyra was moved by default to a household with her father, where she was killed. However, if we consider what the housing department actually did in this case, the judgment seems very harsh. Communications from the Social Services Department were poor. Just over a month after the social worker's first representations, the housing department offered Claudette a flat, which she accepted; but it was too far away from her mother, and Claudette and her family continued to live with Beatrice even though she was formally the tenant of her own flat. I am not sure the housing department had been told enough at this stage to know that the new arrangement was not satisfactory. When, after some time, the social worker took up the case again, she argued for a transfer for Claudette, and a move for her mother. The housing manager accepted the case for priority, though even here, it is not clear that he was told all the facts by the social worker:

> Peter [the housing officer] said he could consider a management transfer for Claudette, especially as she could have a two bedroomed flat; there is a much better chance of 4 bed for Mrs Henry, and he will consider this as a priority (p.56).

Beatrice, the grandmother, was made two offers of four-bedroomed property, one in February 1984, and one in May. The offers were not considered suitable because they would not have met the other main need — to allow Claudette to live nearby so that she could maintain contact with Tyra and could be tested as a mother. Meanwhile, Claudette was going to the Homeless Persons Unit for rehousing, despite having a flat of her own.

> Mr Hall is waiting to hear back from the HO at 20 Taylor if she has relinquished the tenancy. We might still be able to help her under sons and dtrs [*the special scheme to help sons and daughters of tenants*]. This would obviously be much better for appl. as we will see her as intentional [*i.e. intentionally homeless*] ... (p.58).

The impression I have from this is that allocations were fettered by rules which were inappropriate to the particular circumstances; the housing officer responsible tried, to his credit, to interpret these rules flexibly in order to meet the family's needs as best he could. The problem was not that the housing department did not respond; it was that it was not able to respond appropriately.

The substance of the inquiry's complaint, and one which I think is justified in principle even if there is scope to disagree about the details, is that the borough of Lambeth was responsible for the child, and housing could have made a major positive contribution in this case.

While social services may legitimately complain that they got no proper response from housing, and housing that it got no formal priority claim from social services, it is the local authority corporately which bears the responsibility for providing the accommodation and maintenance needed to protect a child in its care. ...it is scandalous that Lambeth was unable to provide one of its own dwellings to enable Beatrice Henry to do the council's own job of keeping Tyra safe and well (ibid, pp. 85; 123).

This point is liable to be met in housing departments by the obvious rejoinder, that the fact that housing and social services were part of the same authority is coincidental; in most parts of the country, it would not be true. But this is to confuse a legal technicality with a principle. If the aim of the welfare state is to provide, to any degree, a comprehensive service, then housing services should be attempting to deal with the sort of conditions which centrally concern Social Services departments. The question of who is legally responsible is a quibble. What matters is what gets done.

Part 4
Housing management

Chapter 12
Housing need

Summary. Housing agencies have traditionally worked with a very narrow definition of 'housing need', based on factors which can be objectively assessed with reasonable ease. This has been shaped by practical constraints on housing management. The case is made for an extension of the concept of housing need to consider the special circumstances of groups requiring community care.

If housing is a social service, then one of the prime tests by which it has to be judged is the extent to which it meets the needs of the people it serves. These needs have to be viewed, not solely in terms of housing conditions, but in the context of a wider understanding of the importance of housing — housing as a commodity in itself, and housing as a determinant of lifestyle. In many ways, the traditional concept of need to which housing management has responded has been far too limited.

It is difficult to define the idea of need clearly. In part, this is true simply because definition is a difficult activity in itself. Everyone knows what a 'house' is, but it is not easy to define a 'house' in a way that accurately describes the meaning of the word, includes all the cases which can reasonably be described as 'houses', and excludes everything which cannot be. In the case of 'need', the problem is made more difficult because the idea is an abstract one; because it refers to several different types or classes of thing — needs can be physical, mental, emotional, material, spiritual; and because of the strength of the appeal associated with the concept. A person who says 'I need' something is not usually making a dispassionate observation; the identification of need is often a powerful emotive claim to have the need met.

'In a general sense', Feinberg writes,

> to say that S needs X is to say simply that if he doesn't have X he will be harmed (1973, p.111).

This will not quite do as a definition of need. People can be harmed by losing something they do not 'need', if the loss is harmful to their interests. But Feinberg is right to point out that there is an implication of harm: people 'need' something, not simply because they are worse off without it, but because there are negative consequences which follow from the lack of the item. People need, for example, shelter or food. A person without these things will suffer negative effects. People without food die, or at least suffer ill health. People without shelter suffer discomfort, illness, and social isolation. It can sometimes be difficult to distinguish negative effects from the absence of positive ones: if a child 'needs' education, this may be seen as much as a comment on the positive benefits of education as on the negative effects of the lack of it. But a positive benefit whose absence has no obvious negative effects, like, say, the lack of a video recorder, cannot be considered a 'need'. Items of this sort are referred to as 'luxuries', though there is often some contention as to just which items should be seen as luxuries, and whether negative effects are incurred by their absence.

The other main point to be drawn from Feinberg's statement is that a need must be a need *for* something. A person may suffer harm, for example as a result of an accident, but it is difficult to identify this as a ground for 'need' in itself; the only 'needs' would be measures either to avoid the harm initially or to alleviate it subsequently. A person who is required to move during a clearance programme is harmed by the fact of having to move in itself; but it would be odd to say that the person therefore 'needed' to stay in the same place. We can say that the person's need is either to have the house improved, or to be offered suitable alternative accommodation. Effectively, the idea of 'need' is subject to interpretation according to the measures available to meet it.

Who defines need?

Bradshaw (1972) distinguishes four kinds of need: normative; comparative; felt; and expressed.

Normative need is defined by a norm, generally established by experts. One example in housing policy is the statutory standard of overcrowding, which defines when a household can be said to be overcrowded: a family with seven children in a two bedroom house might not be overcrowded, whereas a couple in a bedsit may be. Another example is the standard of unfitness, a norm which is vaguer than the standard of overcrowding but which nevertheless defines specific criteria by which a house is to be judged.

Comparative need is defined by comparison with others; people are deemed to be in 'need', for practical purposes, if others have something which they do not. One example of this is the 'General Needs Index' used by central government to distribute resources between local authorities. Priorities in health and personal social services are equally determined, at least in part, on 'indicators' of need. At the individual level, an obvious example is the assessment of need for the allocation of council housing; people receive priority according to the level of need they have.

Although the idea of 'comparative need' is widely used in the distribution of some kinds of resources, it is not an obvious principle. In the health service, a person with two broken legs does not necessarily receive priority over someone else who has only broken one; in social security, the view that people with less resources should be given greater priority is often condemned because of its association with means-testing.

Felt need is felt by the people in need themselves; *expressed* need is what people say they need. The categories of normative need and comparative need are defined by some external arbiter, someone who is not one of the people in need. The contrast of these ideas with 'felt' and 'expressed' need serves to draw attention to the question of who defines need as constituting a claim for service. There are cases in which expert assessment outweighs individual judgment. The most important are those where people are considered unable to exercise a responsible choice — children are required to attend school, and mentally ill people may be committed to institutions for medical treatment — but there are other examples without this qualification, like the fluoridation of water supply in order to reduce dental caries.

If 'need' depends on the degree of suffering someone experiences, it may be difficult to assess from the outside, and there is an argument to say that felt need should be taken into account in attributing priority between competing claims. An example of the kind of conflict which may arise can be found in applications for rehousing. Should a person who suffers depression or stress as a result of insecurity or poor housing conditions be given priority over someone else who does not? This would usually be considered inequitable in housing allocations, because it would penalise those who attempt to cope with equally unsatisfactory conditions, and few if any allocation schemes would take account of it (Spicker 1987). The main cause of homelessness is the breakdown of relationships in the previous accommodation; the failure to take stress into account may arguably have found an outlet in applications for rehousing by homeless people.

The argument that individuals are the best judges of their own needs may be extended to the view that need has to be 'expressed' by the person who has it. 'Expressed' need is a direct claim for priority. However, as Bradshaw points out, this is not directly equivalent to 'felt' need; a person may feel a need without expressing it, and may express a need without feeling it. A reliance on 'expressed' need puts the onus on the individual to claim a service, which is the normal pattern in British social services. Social security benefits have to be claimed (and, notoriously, people are not in general informed of what they might claim); people have to apply for council housing; sick people have to present themselves in order to receive medical care. This can be defended from the point of view of individual freedom — people should not be forced to have services that they do not want. But there are arguments against this method of establishing need. The expression of need assumes that people know the service is available to them; the evidence from social security benefits is that they may not. People may be deterred by the cost or inconvenience of applying for services. And many people are reluctant to claim. For whatever reasons, nearly a third of those entitled to Income Support and over half those entitled to Family Credit do not receive them; and in the health service, a model of universal care accessible to all, those in the lower social classes receive less service despite a greater incidence of serious illness (DHSS 1980). In a recent criticism of local authority waiting lists, a government report draws the extraordinary conclusion that waiting lists overestimate need because many of the people on the lists are not actively seeking housing (DoE 1988). This rests on a confusion between demand and need. The lists may overestimate demand; whether or not they overstate need is another issue entirely.

Housing need

Conventionally, social housing is concerned with 'housing need'. This was formerly a fairly limited concept: a 1949 report commented that:

> in all but a very few cases, housing need arises from one or more of the following factors:
> overcrowding
> ill-health
> lack of a separate home
> other unsatisfactory conditions of an applicant's present accommodation
> (CHAC, 1949, para. 15).

There is still a tendency in some housing departments to refer to 'need' primarily in terms of the size and condition of houses: applicants for transfer from the worst council property are likely to be told that they are satisfactorily housed. The Cullingworth report attempted to expand the concept substantially:

> a person in housing need is simply one who has a need for housing different from that which he currently occupies (CHAC 1969, p.102);

and argued:

> In our view it is not sufficient that local authorities should give priority to 'housing need' as measured by objective factors such as overcrowding, sharing and the like.... (p.21)
> ... the assessment of need must take account of two major factors:
> (i) what are the present housing conditions of the household? — space (too little or too much),; fitness; amenities; design factors; location factors ...; cost; security of tenure ...;
> (ii) how well can this household cope with living in these conditions?' (p.38)

This seems to me to represent a fairly widespread understanding of the idea of 'housing need' in principle. However, even if this limited concept was taken as the standard, there are factors within it commonly not taken into account. Social factors are not universally accepted. It used to be the case that few local authorities took the condition of property into account in their allocation schemes on the basis that housing in bad condition would be dealt with by the clearance programme. Currently, hardly any local authorities consider the financial status of the tenants despite the basically selective approach which is adopted. There are one or two which have income limits (e.g. Croydon and Maidenhead), but they are few and far between. The Cullingworth report argued as follows:

> Different economic and social situations in which different families live must also be taken into account. We are not suggesting that more affluent council tenants should be evicted or that council housing should be reserved for the poor. ... Our point is simply that in allocating council houses local authorities should give particular attention to those with incomes which are low in relation to their needs (CHAC 1969, p.21).

The basic case for taking money into account is that access to adequate housing in the long term is primarily determined by financial resources. Money is, then, a powerful indicator of need — objective, measurable and relatively easy to identify. There are strong arguments against means testing. In the first place, people's income is likely to change in the future and that present circumstances are not necessarily the best indicator of need, but one could say the same about their housing status. Secondly, means tests are seen as stigmatising. Thirdly, housing has become, for many people, a means-tested benefit anyway. The majority of tenants are on housing benefit, not least because anyone with a greater command of resources has more to gain by buying under current financial arrangements. I think these are sound objections; but they are not so devastating that they explain why means-testing should scarcely be used at all.

The idea of 'housing need' is based, in part, on a convention — a widespread use, marking the shared perceptions of housing officers. But it is more than this. Housing need, like any other type of need, is a need for something. The idea of housing need has developed as an operational concept, that is, a concept which was intended to be useful in a particular context. If there is the intention to make some provision, the definition is liable to be more restrictive than if the situation is considered in the abstract. In part, this happens because good housing is in short supply, and a narrower definition of need helps housing officers to ration scarce resources. It also happens, though, because the types of need which actually can be met are limited. It is quite easy to see that if nearly all the houses in Britain were air conditioned, this would be taken into account in allocating houses to certain people with medical and respiratory conditions. But very few houses in Britain are air-conditioned, and virtually none of the houses that people will be allocated are, so the ability to benefit from air conditioning is not considered in calculating someone's need.

The restrictions that are put on the idea of housing need are there because the idea has been shaped by the conditions in which housing officers work. At first sight, some of the restrictions seem strange. Cure takes priority over prevention. A family which is living with parents or friends is likely to become homeless, but this receives less emphasis in many allocations schemes than the number of bedrooms available to a family while it is on the waiting list. People who live in damp housing are less likely to receive consideration for this, despite the evident risk to health, than a person who has to use an outside toilet. This has implications for Social Services recommendations: a social worker concerned with a family 'at risk' is unlikely to receive a sympathetic hearing for a problem which cannot be proved to exist.

It is not surprising that this should have become true. Housing authorities have never been in a position to meet every need. There is enormous pressure for housing; the response has been to take factors which can be proved. The emphasis has been on fairness — on factors which can be assessed and proved. At the same time, the capacity of housing departments to assess needs have been limited. The trend has been to provide simple, easily calculable indicators of need that can reasonably be met. There is, in housing departments, an 'ideology of need' which represents an adjustment to organisational constraints. (This argument is developed more fully in Spicker 1987.)

Meeting needs

In many ways, this book is an argument for the extension of the traditional concept of housing need. In the first place, it is not really possible to separate out an idea of 'housing need' which is distinct from other types of kinds or needs. Housing plays a major part in people's lives. It shapes not only their physical environment, but also their life style and their social relationships. This is not to deny that the traditional forms of housing need still exist, nor that there are other, developing kinds. Needs are complex and many-faceted. However, the problems posed by the groups which have been considered in this book are particularly complex. Because, in general, they are liable to require some degree of support in their accommodation, housing provision alone cannot effectively meet their needs. A mentally handicapped person discharged from an institution, an old person who cannot go out, or a child leaving care, are not adequately served if they are simply rehoused and nothing more is done. Equally, many other needs cannot be met without the contribution of housing services. A mentally ill person who requires accommodation close to an out-patient clinic, a family in which a child is at risk, a disabled person who relies on family support, are all legitimate subjects for consideration by social housing agencies.

Secondly, housing is part of the welfare state, a network of services intended to meet needs as comprehensively as possible, and to the best possible standard. The role of social housing has to be reconsidered in the light of the aims of the welfare state. But it is not possible to assess the contribution of any service in isolation from others. The need for social housing has to be seen in the context of needs and provision overall.

This sounds fine enough in theory. In practice, the approach is beset with problems. Within the housing services themselves, there are difficulties not only from practices and approaches entrenched within the profession of housing management, but a number of deep-rooted structural problems. Housing managers have to deal with a range of conflicting aims; meeting the needs of dependent groups are only a part. They have also to deal with the needs and the legitimate aspirations of existing tenants. There is increasing pressure from the needs and demands of other groups, like homeless people and single people, who have no adequate alternatives beyond social housing. And these pressures have to be balanced in the context of extremely limited resources, political disfavour, and a legacy of major problems.

Even if none of this were true, co-ordination between services to meet needs would face further significant obstacles. There are strong conflicts and rivalries between services, stemming perhaps in part from the contrasting professional traditions, but more importantly from the differing constraints on, and aims of, the different services. There are major administrative obstacles to co-ordination — diverse administrative structures with different boundaries, rules and procedures, and (possibly more important) an endemic lack of resources. When it comes to co-ordination of services, or even improved liaison, there is no adequate definition of responsibilities, no clear procedure to follow, and little political guidance.

There is every reason, then, to be pessimistic; and many of the suggestions in this book about co-ordination or liaison may seem naive and even irrelevant in the context of the conditions which practitioners have to work in. There is no question that resources are severely restricted, but that is not, I think, sufficient reason to disregard the importance of the sorts of needs which I have emphasised. There is a strong moral case to attempt to meet the need. The response to need depends, in large part, on an assessment of priority. The groups which I have discussed are not by any means the only groups which suffer from major disadvantages in our society, but they are clearly disadvantaged nevertheless. Provision for them is central to the precepts of the welfare state, and a valuable principle in itself. It follows, I believe, that they should have a high degree of priority. The difficulty of doing what is right is not a good enough reason not to try.

At the same time, the practical difficulties of serving these groups should not be overestimated; it is difficult, but not impossible. If any public resources are available for the expansion of social housing, they have been most freely available in this field; and housing associations in particular have taken a considerable initiative in drawing on finance from other social services. But housing agencies have two significant resources of their own, which have not always been deployed adequately in the provision of service to those most in need. One is the existing housing stock, which can often be used more flexibly and imaginatively, as it has been in the development of cluster homes for mentally ill or mentally handicapped people. The other resource is the housing officer, whose professional role is gradually being adapted to meet a complex range of needs.

Chapter 13
The role of housing management

Summary. Housing management has relied on the outmoded traditions of estates management, and the paternalism of Octavia Hill. The changing conditions of housing management call for a different set of approaches, with specialised skills in dealing with people with particular needs, and co-operation within a multidisciinary team.

The problems outlined in this book have important implications for the development of housing management. Social housing developed as mass housing, and housing management developed in response, primarily as a service which was concerned with the maintenance and administration of the housing stock. Housing management has been, in the past, a practical function, until fairly recently lacking in status and even now at the margins of 'professional' activity. Wilensky (1964) identifies the following steps in professionalisation:

1. full-time activity at the task
2. the establishment of university training
3. formation of a national professional organisation
4. redefinition of the core task
5. conflict between old timers and new practitioners
6. competition between the new occupation and related ones
7. political pressure to gain legal protections
8. a code of ethics.

Housing management has passed through a number of these stages, but it is still in the process of defining its role, seeking to steer a course between the technical approach of the surveying profession, and the human skills of the personal social services.

One principal influence on the development of housing management has been the school of 'estates management'. Estates management is linked in part with commerce, and an emphasis on financial control, and in part with surveying, which has been primarily concerned with the physical condition of housing rather than the circumstances of tenants.

The influence of this approach can be seen in the common emphasis on the administration of housing rather than the needs of tenants. For example, Macey and Baker's definition of tenants' 'need' is conceived almost wholly in terms of the size and amenities of the property (Macey 1984). So, a frequent response made to tenants who wish to be transferred from one three-bedroomed house to another in a better area is, 'you are satisfactorily housed'.

The main counterbalance to this approach has been the legacy of Octavia Hill (Spicker 1985). Octavia Hill represents, at least, a tradition of housing management as a form of social service, but the work has little else directly to commend it. She took an individualistic, pathological view of the problems of tenants; she gave them a chance to 'improve' or she threw them out. The influence of her disciples can still be seen in a number of ways. One is the exaggerated emphasis in housing management on the importance of rent arrears, leading to problems for people who are homeless because of financial hardship, and difficulties in obtaining transfers. There is the largely misplaced faith which housing officers have in notices to quit and eviction as the main sanction against tenants — the problems are referred to in chapter 4. Another example is the survival of 'housing welfare', where lady investigators inspect the housekeeping standards of tenants and supervise those who fail to maintain an appropriate degree of cleanliness on a regular basis. The treatment of 'problem families' reflects a pathological, individualistic view of poverty. Finally, there is the emphasis on the selection of the 'deserving poor' from those who are 'undeserving'. Octavia Hill's work attracts a level of sustained admiration which is hard to explain (see e.g. Power 1987). Taken in all, she has been a baneful influence on housing management.

The criticisms made of the traditional pattern of housing management have been trenchant. 'Council housing,' Short writes, 'is a paternalistic housing type in which households are visited, selected and allocated dwellings by the housing managers, who set the rents, decide the colour of their doors and determine the rules and regulations which cover tenancy agreements' (1982, p.171). Until the 'tenant's charter' in the 1980 Housing Act, it was commonplace for councils to impose a huge range of conditions on tenants in order to control the way they lived. The National Consumer Council (1976) gives a number of examples. The tenancy agreements include some conditions which are quite justifiable, either because they protect the property (like limitations on structural alterations) or because they reflect planning regulations. But the conditions described also put petty restrictions on people's lives. The rules in the authority where I worked stated that no-one in a council house should have two pets. The justifications for regulations of this sort have usually been based either in the protection of the council's investment in the stock, or in terms of the maintenance of harmonious relationships between tenants. To take a small illustration, it is notorious that in many areas tenants have not been at liberty to paint their own front doors. I've been told that this is a necessary precaution against tenants who would otherwise use industrial paint and make decoration in future difficult. Macey and Baker specifically refer to the issue in respect of *interior* decoration, but reassure us that:

nowadays there are comparatively few cases where amateur efforts on the part of the tenant cause any real damage to the property (1973, p.302).

It is not really worthwhile to go deeply into the question of how many people would damage the property by painting it; it seems more important to ask whether this can ever be a sufficient reason to deny people the opportunity to live in their own homes as they choose.

Paternalistic, Gallagher argues, 'is not a true description: "oppressive" and "regulatory" would be more accurate.' (1982, p.122). In extreme cases, the regulation of tenants' lives can be seen as a form of social control. When a housing welfare officer arrives weekly to encourage someone to clean, when notice is served for failure to maintain a garden, when visitors step in to arbitrate on disputes between neighbours, this can all be seen as a form of control, pressuring tenants to conform to dominant social norms. Probably the best-known example of this is the grading of tenants by their standards of housekeeping and the 'type' of person they are. Macey still advises that 'the personal suitability of the tenant and his wife are a guide to the type of property to be offered' (1982, p.313). One justification for this is, from the point of view of estates management, to protect the most valuable property from the depredations of the worst tenants. Another is the maintenance of harmony on settled estates. Gray strongly identifies grading, and in particular the use of certain estates for 'problem' tenants, with social control:

> Ghetto estates may be viewed as a form of punishment, a device for the disciplining and the social control of other tenants, a means of legitimating managerial assumptions and activities, and providing scapegoats for a variety of issues (Gray 1979, p.226).

There are, certainly, elements of both paternalism and social control in housing management. Much of it is indefensible; but there *is* a case for both, in so far as they increase the welfare of applicants and tenants. As Marshall writes:

> it would be dishonest to pretend that there is not about welfare policy decisions something intrinsically authoritarian or ... paternalistic (1981, p.109).

Social control may be necessary to protect communities. People do care, and care reasonably, what their neighbours are like and how they behave. A degree of control may also be necessary to protect people who are disadvantaged. The justification for the eviction of tenants for racial harassment, for example, is that the right of the person who is being harassed outweighs the right of the tenant to remain in the property. This control ceases to be justifiable where it creates or reinforces disadvantage — as it has done in the case of 'sink' estates.

'Paternalism', similarly, is a pejorative word, but it represents a strongly felt set of beliefs. Paternalistic policies are sometimes justified on the grounds that experts are likely to know better, that people behave unreasonably, or that they are ill placed to make their own decisions. None of this can reasonably be applied to council tenants. But there are two other justifications that might be. One is that people should not have to be bothered with certain decisions or tasks. Certain tenants' co-operatives make a large feature of attendance at meetings — in fact, people may not be allocated houses if they don't attend. This is an intolerable burden to place on people who don't have a sufficient choice as to their accommodation; people have other things to do with their time. It is applying a different standard to disadvantaged people than to others in society. There's a curious idea abroad in some co-operatives that somehow it is more virtuous for poor people to do things themselves than to have things done for them. This seems to go back to the Victorian values of Samuel Smiles and 'Self-Help'.

Secondly, paternalism may increase people's command over their lives. Freedom is not only negative freedom, the absence of interference; it includes positive freedom, the power to act. Poverty restricts freedom, because it limits a person's power to choose, and the provision of housing resources is an important way to reduce poverty. Paternalism may increase a person's power to choose, not only by freeing the person from unnecessary tasks, but by establishing the material foundations necessary to live reasonably independently.

This implies the limits to paternalism. Essentially, paternalism is justified in so far as it is morally right; but self-determination and democracy are also moral principles, to be valued and balanced against others. The position from which I begin is a primary concern with poverty and disadvantage. The paternalism of social housing management, like social control, seems to me justifiable to the extent that it protects those who are most disadvantaged, and unjustified at the point where it begins to reinforce or create disadvantage.

It is clearly important for housing managers to respect the rights of applicants and tenants. A rented house is the tenant's home. The tenant has the right to security, privacy, the use and enjoyment of the property; and tenants' homes should enable them to participate in the same kinds of activities as other people do in their own homes, whether publicly or privately owned. These rights must substantially limit the scope of housing managers for intervention; but in some cases they demand positive action to be protected. The main criticism I would wish to make of housing management is not that it has intervened too much, but that its interventions have often been inappropriate, and have failed adequately to safeguard the interests of applicants and tenants. There is a strong case for more active intervention, for service without waiting to be asked, and, above all, for the protection of the interests and rights of disadvantaged people.

The changing conditions of housing management

Housing management has had to change, because the circumstances in which it operates are changing. Some of these changes are essentially organisational. It would be premature to suppose that local authorities will cease to act as social landlords within the near future, but it is equally clear that they are no longer to be seen as the sole or even the primary form of social housing management. Housing associations are developing as models of the comprehensive housing service. Within the housing association movement, there is a wide range of different types of organisation, including not only those which depend on housing management, as it is traditionally understood, but other initiatives such as co-operatives, hostels, equity sharing, and experiments in special housing. Within the local authorities, there is an increasing emphasis on planning and administration. Local authorities have a range of indirect functions, additional to the direct provision of housing. These indirect functions include the supervision of standards in the rented sector, the planning of strategies to meet housing need, and the development of initiatives, and the administration of Housing Benefit (which must be seen in itself as a major element in the functioning of the rented sector).

Housing managers are being faced with an expanding set of problems, which demand an ever wider range of skills and areas of knowledge and competence. The ideal of a 'comprehensive housing service' seems more and more impossible to achieve. It was possible to imagine that one profession might be responsible for the basic functions of managing the housing stock: supervision of construction, allocations, tenancy relations, rent collection, and maintenance. This in turn required an expansion of the functions of administration, research, planning and finance, competencies which are increasingly expected of any senior estates manager or officer of a housing association. But housing management is not only about managing properties; it is also about dealing with people. And the sort of problems which housing managers are now being expected to cope with include not only the general functions associated with responding to applicants and tenants, but people with major problems, and to make an appropriate response often requires highly developed skills.

The pattern of training in housing management has been based on a generic model of comprehensive management. It is a fallacy to suppose that, if a comprehensive housing service is to be provided, it must be provided by one person equipped comprehensively with all the skills necessary for good management. Certainly, housing managers need a basis of generic skills. They include, on one side, the skills associated with 'estates management' — administration, accounting, personnel management, negotiation, report writing — and knowledge of principles of management, construction, law, finance, research and planning. For the management of relationships with tenants, housing managers also require a range of interpersonal skills, including interviewing, assessment and communication, and being prepared to give personal support to people under stress.

However, this generic foundation is increasingly inadequate to deal with the level and severity of the problems which housing managers face. In respect of estates management, many housing managers find themselves ill-prepared from their professional training to instruct architects, to negotiate costs, to steer an innovative development past planning authorities, or to forecast demand from demographic trends. In dealing with tenants, few housing managers are equipped by their training to deal adequately with a discharged psychiatric patient who has no support in the community, to be a resource for a group of mentally handicapped people, to identify the signs of stress which may lead to violence. In all these cases, housing managers are expected to 'learn from experience' — a phrase which may well mean 'sink or swim'. These are all areas which people can be trained for, which are trained for in other professions, and in which training does lead to a higher standard of practice in the field: surveyors are generally equipped for the former set of tasks, and social workers for the latter. The difference is that housing managers are supposed to do it all, which is frankly ridiculous.

As housing management develops, it is becoming increasingly clear that many specialisms are being maintained even within the 'comprehensive' housing service. Surveyors have long been recognised as being able to offer a distinctive contribution to estates management. Housing associations are increasingly hiring financial managers or accountants to cope with the mind-boggling complexity of arrangements for public and private finance. The disadvantage of a pure specialism is that it can lead to a narrow focus, ignoring other aspects of the work. But what would be possible, and what would make sense, is for housing managers to specialise after acquiring a generic foundation. After an initial training in a broad range of skills, and acquiring knowledge of the range of activities undertaken, housing managers would then learn the skills and develop the competencies appropriate to particular roles and tasks. The comprehensive housing service can be provided, not by a superhuman individual, but by a management team consisting of people with a range of specialisms and skills appropriate to the needs of the organisation as a whole. This is the likely direction of housing management in the future.

The organisational changes in housing management reflect changes in the perceived purposes of social housing. They have less to do with shifts in government policy than with broader changes in society. The problems which face British housing now are very different from the problems of the 1930s. Mass housing developed as a response to mass housing problems. Relatively few houses now are unfit. In housing policy, the issues which matter now are access, location, finance, social conditions, and the environment. This is not to say that the traditional problems of unfitness, overcrowding and squalor do not still exist; but they are very different to what they used to be, and are differently conceived. The demands which are being made of social housing are very different from what once they were. It is evident that rented housing is not the first choice of most people looking for decent housing, and that social housing is not capable in its present form of meeting many people's aspirations for improving physical and social circumstances. One of the major problems facing housing managers now is how, within the constraints of social housing, to deal with the aspirations of the tenants who they have traditionally catered for — tenants who have been rehoused through general needs, whose standard of living has improved, and who have the option or who have the reasonable expectation of a standard equivalent to those of owner-occupation. Equally, social housing has also to deal with the reasonable aspirations of tenants who are poor, who are denied any other opportunity of improvement. The central principle is a recognition of the importance of housing for the welfare of tenants, applicants and others — the clients of housing management — and of the ways in which housing might be used for their benefit.

Conclusion: a new approach to housing management

This book has been concerned with a set of principles, deriving mainly from the role of housing as a social service in the context of a welfare state; a range of problems, including the problems of poverty and dependency; and a number of responses which can be made to them. Taken together, these issues form the basis of a different kind of approach to housing management, a model which is not 'new' or 'original', because I think it genuinely reflects the developing practice of an increasing number of housing officers in the field, but one which has rarely been expressed in the literature on housing management. The core of this model is a view of social housing as a crucial element in the welfare state, not only because of its importance as a physical commodity, but because housing is central to people's social lives. In work with their clients, housing officers have to take a broad view of their needs, recognising the problems of disadvantage at the individual level, the importance of their social situation, and the potential which housing has to bring about or facilitate changes. The responsibilities of housing officers extend beyond responses to individuals in need, to include carers, and the needs of the wider society in the attempt to improve welfare. Social housing provides an important service, not only in the provision of 'bricks and mortar', but increasingly in levels of welfare support; and housing officers often occupy an important position as primary contacts with their clients. Housing management requires not only a commitment to welfare, but an improved knowledge of individual and social conditions, and increased skills in dealing with these conditions (sometimes on a specialised basis).

However, neither housing management nor the needs of its clients can be seen in isolation. In the past, housing officers have been able to function in a fairly independent manner, doing their bit while other agencies did theirs. The idea that accommodation can be separated from 'support' stems from this approach. But the nature of the problems which are being dealt with means that, in many cases, the separation is artificial and potentially counter-productive. The response to the needs of disadvantaged people has to be made in conjunction with other services and other kinds of responses. At the level of policy, this calls for agreed priorities and the development of organisational and financial structures which make co-ordination possible. Organisationally, there is a need for an agreed division of labour with a clear specification of roles and responsibilities, commonly defined geographical areas or 'patches', and liaison and co-ordination through the development of multidisciplinary teams. From the point of view of service provision, there has to be a range of available responses, allowing appropriate responses to be selected according to the needs of the individuals or groups. In practice, there has to be knowledge and understanding of the roles and contexts of other professionals in other services, direct liaison between people with operational responsibility, and co-operation with multidisciplinary teams.

The dominant model of housing management has to become not maintenance of the housing stock but service to disadvantaged people and the wider community, in co-operation with others. It was always a difficult task. But this shift now has to be made with reduced resources, greater concentrations of poverty and deprivation, and the problems of maintaining a declining housing stock. The issue of resources is crucial to any improvement. The Priority Estates Projects have shown that the intensive management of some estates, with specific budgets for the estates, has been able to change conditions in depressed estates. 'Almost all projects', Anne Power comments, 'had a better repairs service, a better environment, greater security, more involvement with residents and successful physical improvements' (1984, p.32). It is as well to remember, however, that none of these projects succeeded in improving conditions in every area of concern. It would be surprising, in view of the depth and severity of the social conditions in which housing management operates, if they could.

References

Abel-Smith B 1976 Value for money in health services, Heinemann, London

Alinsky S 1971 Rules for radicals: a practical primer for realistic radicals, Random House, New York

Arber S, Gilbert N, Evandrou M, 1988 Gender, household composition and receipt of domiciliary services by the elderly disabled. Journal of Social Policy 17(2) pp. 153-176

Atkinson A B, 1969 Poverty in Britain and the reform of social security, Cambridge University Press.

Atkinson D, 1988 Residential care for children and adults with mental handicap. NISW, Residential care: the research reviewed. HMSO

Audit Commission 1984 Bringing council tenants' arrears under control. HMSO

Audit Commission 1986 Managing the crisis in council housing. HMSO

Bailey R, Brake M (eds) 1975 Radical social work. Arnold, London

Barclay P M et al 1982 Social workers: their role and tasks. Bedford Square Press, London

Barnes J, Lucas H, 1975 Positive discrimination in education. In Barnes J (ed) Educational Priority. vol.3, HMSO

Barton R 1976 Institutional neurosis. Wright (3rd ed.)

Bayley M 1973 Mental Handicap and Community Care. RKP, London.

Becker S, MacPherson S (eds) 1988 Public issues, private pain. Insight

Beckerman W, Clark S 1982 Poverty and social security in Britain since 1961. Oxford University Press, Oxford

Black J, Bowl R Burns D, Critcher C, Grant G, Stockford D, 1983 Social work in context: a comparative study of three social services teams. Tavistock, London.

Blacker C P (ed), 1952 Problem families: five inquiries Eugenics Society

Blaxter M 1974 Health 'on the welfare' — a case study. Journal of Social Policy 3(1), pp.39-51

Blaxter M 1976 The meaning of disability: a sociological study of impairment. Heinemann, London

Blom-Cooper L et al 1985 A child in trust. London Borough of Brent

Booth T, Berry S 1984 An overdose of care. Community Care. 26th July

Borsay A 1986 Disabled people in the community: a study of housing, health and welfare services, Bedford Square Press, London

Bowlby J 1951 Maternal care and mental health. WHO, Geneva

Bradshaw J 1972 A taxonomy of social need. In MacLachlan G (ed) Problems and progress in medical care (7th series). Oxford University Press, Oxford

Brewer C, Lait J 1980 Can social work survive? Temple Smith, London

Briggs A 1961 The welfare state in historical perspective. European Journal of Sociology 2, pp.221-258

Brown J C 1984 Disability income, part II: the disability income system. Policy Studies Institute

Brown G W, Harris T 1978 Social origins of depression: a study of psychiatric disorder in women. Tavistock, London

Brown M, Madge N 1982 Despite the welfare state. Heinemann, London

Burnett J 1978 A social history of housing 1815-1970. David and Charles

Byrne A, Padfield C F 1985 Social services made simple (3rd ed). W H Allen

Cantle T 1986 The deterioration of public sector housing. In Malpass P (ed) The housing crisis. Croom Helm

Central Housing Advisory Committee 1949 Selection of tenants. Ministry of Health, London

Central Housing Advisory Committee 1969 Council housing: purposes, priorities and procedures. HMSO.

CPRS: Central Policy Review Staff 1975 A joint framework for social policies. HMSO.

CPRS 1977 Relations between central government and local authorities. HMSO

Central Statistical Office 1987 Social Trends 17. HMSO

Clapham D, Kintrea K 1986 Rationing, choice and constraint: the allocation of public housing in Glasgow. Journal of Social Policy. vol. 15

Cmd. 6404 1942 Social insurance and allied services (the Beveridge report). HMSO

Cmd. 6922 1946 Report of the committee on the care of children (Curtis Report). HMSO

Cmnd. 169 1957 Royal Commission on the law relating to mental illness and mental deficiency: report. HMSO

Cmnd. 663 1956 Committee of enquiry into the cost of the National Health Service. HMSO

Cmnd. 1191 1960 Report of the committee on Young Persons (Ingleby report). HMSO

Cmnd. 2306 1964 Children and Young Persons, Scotland. HMSO

Cmnd. 2742 1965 The Child, the Family and the Young Offender. HMSO

Cmnd. 3703 1968 Report of the Committee on Local Authority and Allied Personal Social Services. HMSO

Cmnd. 3795 1969 Report of the committee of enquiry into ... Ely hospital, Cardiff. HMSO

Cmnd. 4040 1969 Royal Commission on Local Government in England: Report. HMSO

Cmnd. 4683 1971 Better Services for the Mentally Handicapped. HMSO

Cmnd. 7357 1978 Report of the committee of inquiry into Normansfield Hospital. HMSO

Cmnd. 7468 1979 Report of the Committee of Enquiry into Mental Handicap Nursing and Care. HMSO

Cmnd. 7615 1979 Royal Commission on the National Health Service: Report. HMSO

Cmnd. 7725 1979 Supplementary Benefits Commission Annual Report 1978. HMSO

Cmnd. 9517 1985 Reform of social security, vol 1. HMSO

Cm 214 1987 Housing: the government's proposals. HMSO

Coleman A 1985 Utopia on Trial: vision and reality in planned housing. Shipman

Collison P, 1963 The Cutteslowe walls: a study in social class. Faber

Craig G 1988 " ... And the wheel of fortune". Community Care. 8th December, iii-iv

Cumming E, Cumming J 1957 Closed ranks: an experiment in mental health education. Harvard University Press, Cambridge, Mass

DHSS: Department of Health and Social Security 1971 Handicapped and Impaired in Great Britain. HMSO

DHSS 1973 Residential accommodation for elderly people, Building Note 2

DHSS 1974 Report of the Committee of Inquiry into the care and supervision of Maria Colwell. HMSO

DHSS 1976a Sharing resources for health in England. HMSO

DHSS 1976b Priorities for health and social services in England. HMSO

DHSS 1976c Prevention and health: everyone's business. HMSO

DHSS 1978 Social assistance: a review of the Supplementary Benefits system in Great Britain. London

DHSS 1979 Patients first. HMSO

DHSS 1980 Inequalities in health. HMSO

DHSS 1981 Report of a Study on Community Care

DoE: Department of the Environment 1988 Queuing for housing: a study of council housing waiting lists. HMSO

Duke C 1970 Colour and rehousing. Institute of Race Relations

Feinberg J 1973 Social philosophy. Prentice-Hall, Englewood Cliffs, NJ

Field F 1976 Killing a commitment: the cabinet versus the children. New Society. 17th June, pp 630-632

Finch J 1984 Education as social policy. Longman, London

Flynn M, Flynn P, Mellor N 1972 Social malaise research: a study in Liverpool. In: Central Statistical Office, Social Trends no 3, HMSO

Forrest R, Murie A 1983 Residualisation and council housing. Journal of social policy, vol. 12

Fox D 1982-1983 Articles in Housing, February 1982, March 1982, September 1983

Gallagher P 1982 Ideology and housing management. In: English J (ed) The future of council housing. Croom Helm

Gibbons J 1988 Residential care for mentally ill adults. In: National Institute for Social Work, Residential care: the research reviewed. HMSO

Goffman E 1961 Asylums. Penguin, Harmondsworth 1968

Goldberg E M, Connolly N 1983 The effectiveness of social care for the elderly. Heinemann

Goldberg E M, Warburton R 1979 Ends and means in social work. Allen and Unwin

Gray F 1979 Consumption: council house managers. In: Merrett S State Housing in Britain. RKP

Griffiths R 1988 Community care: agenda for action. HMSO

Hicks D 1976 Primary Health Care: a review. DHSS

Hill M J 1980 Understanding social policy. Blackwell, Oxford

Hillery G A 1955 Definitions of community: areas of agreement. Rural sociology 20, pp 111-123

House of Commons Social Services Committee 1985 Second report from the Social Services Committee 1984-85: Community Care, vol. 1, HC 13-I

Hudson Barbara 1982 Social Work with psychiatric patients. Macmillan, London

Hudson Bob 1986 In pursuit of co-ordination - housing and the personal social services. Local Government Studies 12(2) pp 53-66

Huttman E D 1969 Stigma and public housing, Ph.D. University of California at Berkeley.

Jones K 1972 A History of the Mental Health Services. RKP

Jones K 1975 Opening the door. RKP

Klein R 1977 Priorities and the problems of planning. British Medical Journal, 22nd October, pp 1096-1097

Labour Party 1964 Crime: a challenge to us all (Longford report). Labour Party.

Laurance J 1988 Top of the health league? New Society 20th May, pp 23-24

Layard R, Piachaud D, Stewart M 1978 The causes of poverty (Royal Commission on the Distribution of Income and Wealth Background Paper no. 5). HMSO

Lee K, Mills A 1982 Policy making and planning in the health sector. Croom Helm

Legrand J 1984 The future of the welfare state. New Society 7th June, pp. 385-386

Lewis O 1968 La vida. Panther

McAuley A N D 1977 Soviet anti-poverty policy 1955-1975. University of Essex Department of Economics

Macey J P, Baker J C V 1973 Housing Management, 2nd ed. Estates Gazette

Macey J P 1982 Housing Management, 4th ed. Estates Gazette

Mack J, Lansley S 1985 Poor Britain. Allen and Unwin

Malin N, Race D, Jones G 1980 Services for the mentally handicapped in Britain. Croom Helm

Marshall T H 1981 The right to welfare. Heinemann

Martin J P 1984 Hospitals in Trouble. Blackwell, Oxford

Meteyard B 1985 When a home is not a home. Community Care, 24th Oct

Miller E J, Gwynne G V 1972 A life apart. Tavistock

Ministry of Pensions and National Insurance 1966 Financial and other circumstances of retirement pensioners. HMSO

Minns R 1972 "Homeless families and some organisational determinants of deviancy. Policy and Politics 1(1)

Morris P 1969 Put away. RKP

National Consumer Council 1976 Tenancy agreements between councils and their tenants. NCC

National Development Group for the Mentally Handicapped 1980 Improving the quality of services for mentally handicapped people. DHSS

National Institute for Social Work 1988 Residential care: the research reviewed. HMSO

Newman O 1973 Defensible space: people and design in the violent city. Architectural Press

Orbach L F 1977 Homes for heroes. Seeley Service

Parker R A 1988 Residential care for children. In: National Institute for Social Work; Residential care: the research reviewed. HMSO

Parton N 1985 The politics of child abuse. Macmillan

Pascall G 1986 Social policy: a feminist analysis. Tavistock

Phillips D L 1963 Rejection: a possible consequence of seeking help for mental disorders. American Sociological Review 28(6), pp.963-972

Phillips D 1966 Public identification and acceptance of the mentally ill. American Journal of Public Health and the Nation's Health. 56(5), pp.755-763

Phillips M H 1981 Favourable family impact as an objective of means support policy. In: Brown P G et al (eds), Income support: conceptual and policy issues. Rowman and Littlefield, Totowa N.J.

Philp A F, Timms, N 1957 The problem of 'the problem family'. Family Service Units

Piachaud D 1973 Taxation and poverty. In: Robson W, Crick, B (eds) Taxation policy. Penguin, Harmondsworth

Piachaud D 1980 Children and poverty. Child Poverty Action Group

PSI: Policy Studies Institute 1984 The reform of Supplementary Benefit: working papers. PSI

Pope N 1988 Outpatients on the scrap heap. Guardian, 30th November, p.25

Powell J E 1966 Medicine and politics. Pitman Medical

Power A 1984 Local housing management: a priority estates project survey. Department of the Environment

Power A 1987 Property before people: the management of 20th century housing. Allen and Unwin

Purkis A, Hodson P 1982 Housing and community care. Bedford Square Press

Reardon M 1988 Training for change. Housing, April, pp 27-31

Rein M 1983 From policy to practice. Macmillan

Reynolds F 1986 The problem housing estate. Gower

Ritchie J, Keegan J 1983 Housing for mentally ill and mentally handicapped people. Department of the Environment, HMSO

Rutter M, Madge N 1976 Cycles of disadvantage. Heinemann

Sainsbury S 1973 Measuring disability. G Bell

Sanford J 1978 Tolerance of debility in elderly dependants by supporters at home. In: Carver V, Liddiard P (eds) An Ageing Population. Hodder and Stoughton

Schorr A L 1964 Slums and social insecurity. Nelson

Scull A 1984 Decarceration: community treatment and the deviant, 2nd edn. Polity Press

Sedley S (chair) et al 1987 Whose child?: the report of the public inquiry into the death of Tyra Henry. London Borough of Lambeth

Segal S P 1978 Attitudes toward the mentally ill: a review. Social Work 23(3), pp. 211-217.

Short J R 1982 Housing in Britain: the post war experience. Methuen

Simpson A 1981 Stacking the decks. Nottingham Community Relations Council

Sinclair I 1988 Residential care for elderly people. In: National Institute for Social Work, Residential care: the research reviewed. HMSO

Slater E, Roth M (eds) 1977 Mayer Gross Slater and Roth: Clinical psychiatry, 3rd ed. Ballière Tindall

Social Services Insight 1988, ADC riled by Griffiths housing suggestion 3(13)

Spicker P 1984 Stigma and social welfare. Croom Helm

Spicker P 1985 The legacy of Octavia Hill. Housing, June

Spicker P 1987 Concepts of need in housing allocation. Policy and Politics 15(1), pp. 17-27

Stopford V 1987 Understanding disability: causes, characteristics and coping. Edward Arnold

Thompson Q 1973 Assessing the need for residential care for the elderly. GLC Intelligence Bulletin 24

Titmuss R M 1955 The social division of welfare: some reflections on the search for equity. In: Essays on "the Welfare State", 2nd ed. George Allen and Unwin, London

Townsend P 1979 Poverty in the United Kingdom. Penguin, Harmondsworth

Tyrell H 1988 Residents in legal battle over home. Nottingham Evening Post, 7th June

Tucker J 1966 Honorable estates. Victor Gollancz

Tudor Hart J 1971 The inverse care law. Lancet, 1

Valentine C A 1968 Culture and poverty. University of Chicago Press

Wagner G et al 1988 Residential care: a positive choice. HMSO

Walker A 1980 The social creation of poverty and dependency in old age. Journal of Social Policy 9(1), pp. 49-75

Walker R, Hedges A 1985 Housing benefit: the experience of implementation. Housing Centre Trust

Walker R, Lawton D 1988 Social assistance and territorial justice: the example of single payments. Journal of Social Policy 17(4), pp. 437-476

Wedge P, Prosser H 1973 Born to fail? Arrow

Wicks M 1978 Old and cold: hypothermia and social policy. Heinemann

Widgery D 1979 Health in danger: the crisis in the NHS. Macmillan

Wilensky H 1964 The professionalisation of everyone. American Journal of Sociology 70, pp. 142-6

Wilson E 1982 Women, community and the family. In: Walker A (ed) Community Care. Blackwell

Wolfensberger W (ed) 1972 The principle of normalisation in human services. National Institute on Mental Retardation, Toronto

Index